John Sykes

111 Places
in London
That You
Shouldn't Miss

Photographs by Birgit Weber

emons:

For Helmut and Birgit

Eisenhower Public Library
4613 N. Oketo Avenue
Harwood Heights, IL   60706
708-867-7828
eisenhowerlibrary.org

MIX
Paper from
responsible sources
FSC® C083411

© Emons Verlag GmbH
All rights reserved
© Photographs: Birgit Weber, except chapter 5, 9, 17,
18, 22, 24, 28, 40, 58 (John Sykes);
chapter 60 courtesy of Marion Macalpine
Design: Eva Kraskes, based on a design
by Lübekke | Naumann | Thoben
Maps: altancicek.design, www.altancicek.de
Basic cartographical information from Openstreetmap,
© OpenStreetMap-Mitwirkende, OdbL
Printing and binding: Grafisches Centrum Cuno, Calbe
Printed in Germany 2021
ISBN 978-3-7408-1168-6
Fully revised new edition, August 2021

Did you enjoy it? Do you want more?
Join us in uncovering new places around the world on:
www.111places.com

Foreword

10/21

We pounded miles of pavements, visiting well over 111 places and taking many thousands of photos, in order to arrive at the selection presented here.

Famous sights like Big Ben and Westminster Abbey are not included. Instead we went to Little Ben and the under-visited Westminster Cathedral. We looked at places that visitors might find on their second or fifth trip to London. Many of them are in inner London, but excursions beyond the city centre to all points of the compass are also included.

We aim to show the breathtaking diversity of a city where all the cultures of the world meet. Its architecture ranges from aristocratic residences to heritage-listed wooden huts, its places of leisure from gentlemen's clubs with strict admission criteria to pubs for everyone, its shops from centuries-old retailers to stores selling in-your-face young fashion. We invite readers to accompany us to a synagogue, a Hindu temple and the Dalai Lama's Tibetan garden. We visit an unconsecrated burial place and a romantically decayed cemetery. We present God's Own Junkyard, the Naked Ladies on the banks of the Thames, a bridge that rolls up, and the wine dealer that weighed its customers.

There is a deliberate gap in the list of 111 places: 110 is followed by 112. Fans of cricket will know the reason for this superstition, and everyone else can read about it in connection with Lord's Cricket Ground (see ch. 58).

We hope that readers who explore London with this book enjoy themselves as much as we did while researching, taking photographs and writing.

John Sykes & Birgit Weber

111 Places

1_ 10 Adam Street

Not Downing Street

It may be the most famous door in the world. It is the stage set for major political announcements: the black-painted entrance to 10 Downing Street. In 2016 David Cameron stood outside and announced his resignation after failing to persuade a majority of voters to stay in the European Union. His predecessor Gordon Brown stood there after losing the election in 2010, the black door and white number 10 visible in the background on the press photos. Margaret Thatcher did the same in 1990, with the door open behind her. Defeat is not, however, the only reason to appear on this spot: Winston Churchill posed here, holding up two fingers in a V for victory.

Since a mortar attack on the building in 1991, the general public have not been admitted to Downing Street to admire the scene, and the original oak has been replaced by blast-proof steel. But if you want to get close to a similar door, you only have to walk a few minutes along Whitehall and The Strand, then turn right into Adam Street and look out for number 10 on the left.

It's not a perfect match. The door in Downing Street is shinier, has a black lion's-head knocker, and seven segments rather than five in its fan light. Above the prime minister's door hangs a lantern, and there are boot-scrapers to left and right. 10 Downing Street has an elegant stone door-case, but lacks the fluted pilasters that flank the impostor in Adam Street. In other words, a practised eye will not be deceived. Nevertheless, at a quick glance, most people won't spot the fake. So don't be shy, it's a great photo opportunity! Walk up to the door, pretend to knock or to enter with an air of confidence and entitlement, and post the result on social media. When your friends ask what's going on, make sure you have rehearsed in your mind what you said to the prime minister and let everybody know about it.

Address 10 Adam Street, WC2N 6HA | **Getting there** Tube to Charing Cross (Bakerloo, Northern Line) | **Hours** View from outside at any time | **Tip** Nearby the brothers John and Robert Adam built Adelphi Terrace, a row of neo-Classical houses with a river view, in 1768–1772. Most were demolished in the 1930s, but no. 11 Adelphi Terrace gives a good impression. To see it, walk down to the end of Adam Street to look down on the Embankment gardens, turn right, then right again into Robert Street.

2 Albert Bridge

A frail old soldier

Tower Bridge may be world-famous, but nothing spans the Thames more beautifully than Albert Bridge a few miles upstream. Named after Queen Victoria's consort, the bridge is truly enchanting after dark, when 4,000 fairy lights put a magic sparkle on its octagonal towers and iron stays. During daylight hours, the pastel shades of its paint – pink, blue and yellow – pick out the intricacies of the structure. The dainty appearance of Albert Bridge is not misleading: ever since its inauguration in 1873, it has given headaches to civil engineers, as its 19th-century nickname, the 'trembling lady' indicates. The historic signs that warned companies of soldiers from nearby Chelsea Barracks to break step as they marched across are still in place.

The engineer Rowland Mason Ordish designed Albert Bridge as his own patented variant of the cable-stayed bridge. It had to be reinforced only 11 years after opening. In the late 1950s, a vigorous campaign by prominent supporters, including the poet John Betjeman, prevented demolition. For the centenary of the bridge in 1973, piers were placed in the river to shore it up. Recent structural problems are connected to the social make-up of the neighbourhood: residents from the north bank drive across in their heavy, four-wheel-drive 'Chelsea tractors', but the brittle cast-iron structure was never intended to carry motorised traffic. They also walk their poodles to Battersea Park on the south bank. As some dogs cannot wait till they reach the other side, urine corrodes the wooden deck beneath the roadway.

Following restoration, Albert Bridge was reopened in 2011, not by royalty but with 'walkies' for Prince and Albert, two residents of Battersea Dogs' Home. A splendid sight but frail with age, like the uniformed veteran soldiers of the nearby Royal Hospital, the bridge stands upright and does its duty.

Address Chelsea Embankment/Cheyne Walk (north side of the bridge) | Getting there Tube to Sloane Square (Circle, District Line); bus 170 from Victoria to Albert Bridge | Tip The Royal Hospital in Chelsea with its beautiful chapel and Great Hall was built by Christopher Wren in 1682 (Royal Hospital Road, for opening hours see www.chelsea-pensioners.co.uk).

3 Angela's Fountain
The gift of a remarkable woman

In Victoria Park in Hackney stands an elaborate octagonal structure in Gothic Revival style: the Burdett-Coutts Memorial Drinking Fountain, a little architectural gem, and an adornment to one of London's loveliest parks, even though water no longer flows. Pillars of red granite support an upper section of light-coloured sandstone and a steep-pitched roof with clock faces on four sides and a weather vane in the shape of a golden mermaid. Around the well chamber, cherubs ride on dolphins. The water used to splash from stone pots into basins of grey granite. Visitors to the park could quench their thirst from metal cups attached by chains.

The fountain was inaugurated in 1862 in front of a crowd of 10,000. Angela Georgina, Baroness Burdett-Coutts (1814–1906), had donated £6000 to provide clean drinking water to the inhabitants of the poor East End. She could afford to be generous, as she had inherited £1.8 million at the age of 23 from her grandfather Thomas Coutts, who had owned a bank. Needless to say, there were many suitors for the hand of the wealthiest heiress in England, but they wooed her in vain. Angela was an independent-minded woman, who preferred to devote her fortune to good causes rather than a husband. The list of projects that she supported is long: a hostel and education for young women whose poverty forced them into prostitution, the London Society for the Prevention of Cruelty to Children, schools, a water supply in Jerusalem and a market in Columbia Road.

When Baroness Burdett-Coutts finally married at the age of 67, polite society was shocked: the lucky man was her 29-year-old private secretary. As he was American-born, according to the terms of her inheritance she lost half of her income – but the marriage was happy. King Edward VII described her as 'the most remarkable woman in the kingdom after my mother (Queen Victoria)'.

Address Victoria Park, Hackney, E3 5TB | Getting there Train from Liverpool Street to Cambridge Heath, then walk along Bishop's Way to the Regent's Canal and across the footbridge into the park | Hours Park: daily 7am – dusk | Tip Refreshments are served in The Hub Café at the centre of the park (daily 9am – 4pm, www.thehubvictoriapark.net).

4 Apothecaries' Hall

A survival from the age of guilds

In the alleys and courts between Ludgate Hill and the Thames, you can still get a feel of a bygone, small-scale London – for example in narrow Black Friars Lane next to a railway viaduct. The friars were Dominicans, whose refectory became a theatre after the dissolution of the monasteries under King Henry VIII. Shakespeare once trod the boards there, in the place now called Playhouse Yard, and bought a house in nearby Ireland Yard. Another part of the Dominicans' premises was taken over in 1632 by the Society of Apothecaries, one of London's 109 'livery companies'.

The livery companies, so called for their ceremonial gowns, originated in the Middle Ages as guilds of tailors, wine merchants, goldsmiths and other occupations. They laid down the rules of their trades, had religious roles and elected the Lord Mayor. Most of them have now become charitable organisations, but some still have professional functions. The Society of Apothecaries possesses the oldest remaining livery hall. Parts of it, including the 18-metre-long Great Hall with its oak panelling, large chandelier and historic portraits of officers of the society, date from 1670. The coat of arms that adorns the modest façade in Black Friars Lane shows Apollo slaying a dragon, the symbol of disease, with a Latin motto meaning 'I am called a bringer of help throughout the world'.

Originally organised within the guild of pepper merchants, the apothecaries founded their own livery company in 1617. Half a century later, they established a botanical garden for growing plants, the Chelsea Physic Garden, which still exists. Past members include the poet John Keats and Elizabeth Garrett Anderson (1836–1917), the first Englishwoman to qualify as a doctor. Until 1922, the Society of Apothecaries ran a pharmaceutical business. Today it holds post-graduate examinations in medicine and awards a prize for medical history. And the senior members still elect the Lord Mayor.

Address Black Friars Lane, EC4V, www.apothecaries.org | Getting there Tube to Blackfriars (Circle, District Line) | Tip As a consolation for the fact that Apothecaries' Hall is rarely open to the public, a nearby pub, The Black Friar on the corner of New Bridge Street, has an opulent interior in the Arts & Crafts style.

5 The Argyll Arms

A refuge from shopping hell

Pushing and jostling along Oxford Street, Londoners and visitors from all over the world engage in a collective retail frenzy. For those who find this place unbearable, and for fashion victims seeking to recuperate after their shopping trip, there is a haven close to Oxford Circus Tube Station in Argyll Street: a pub that is also a gem of interior design.

In the 18th century, the Duke of Argyll resided in the street – the Palladium Theatre now occupies the site – and the sign over the door bears his coat of arms. A tavern has stood here since 1742, but the wonderful interior of the Argyll Arms dates mainly from 1895. This was the golden age of pub architecture when breweries, facing stiffer competition than ever from other places of amusement such as theatres, bought up modest watering holes and turned them into gleaming palaces. They aimed to counter the arguments of the temperance movement by demonstrating taste and decency.

The Argyll Arms is fitted with dark wood, mirrors and etched glass. Three snug screened-off drinking areas lie between a corridor and the long bar. The partitions are made from carved mahogany and frosted glass into which delicate patterns have been etched: floral motifs, cornucopias and vases. Subdued lamplight glows in the dimness, sparkles in the mirrors and lends depth to the patterns in the glass. Above this, painted dark red, is a ceiling of Lincrusta, a deeply embossed material related to linoleum that was used as a wall covering in Victorian times. This ceiling may well be as old as the building, which dates from 1868. To the rear is a rare surviving example of a publican's office, also partitioned off with panels of etched glass and mahogany, and boasting a clock with a carved encasement. As The Argyll Arms is a listed building, its beauty will be preserved for future generations of drinkers and exhausted shoppers.

Address 18 Argyll Street, W1F 7TP | Getting there Tube to Oxford Circus (Bakerloo, Central, Victoria Line) | Hours Daily noon–11pm, Sun until 10pm | Tip Take the Central Line two stops east to Holborn to admire another fine old pub: The Princess Louise (209 High Holborn) with its tiles, mirrors and a historic gents' toilet.

6 The Athenaeum Club

The goddess admits those who are worthy

Among the grey stone façades on Pall Mall and St James's Street, the district of gentlemen's clubs, one club stands out from the others thanks to its bright, cream-coloured paint, a replica of the Parthenon frieze in white on a blue background and a brilliantly gilded female figure, the goddess Athene, who stands above the Doric columns of the entrance with her helmet and spear. Her gaze lowered and left arm outstretched, she seems to be inviting deserving mortals into the club.

In 1824 the writer John Wilson Croker, the artist Sir Thomas Lawrence and other eminent men founded the Athenaeum Club, intending it to be a meeting place for outstanding persons in the fields of science, art and literature. Whereas other clubs appealed to army officers, politicians, travellers or gamblers and drinkers, the Athenaeum was a refuge for intellectuals. The decision to spend money on the expensive Parthenon frieze instead of facilities to cool members' drinks underlined its aspirations, as a satirical verse recorded: 'I'm John Wilson Croker, I do as I please; instead of an ice house I give you – a frieze!' The members have included Joseph Conrad, Rudyard Kipling, J. M. W. Turner, Charles Darwin and, to date, 52 Nobel Prize laureates. The scientist Michael Faraday, whose wheelchair has been preserved in the club, ensured that the rooms had electric lighting as early as 1886. At the foot of the wide staircase Charles Dickens and William Makepeace Thackeray, the latter mortally ill, were reconciled in 1863 after a quarrel that had lasted for years.

Today, government ministers, high-ranking civil servants and bishops are among the members. Women were not admitted until 2002, but now they too can dine and stay overnight in the club, read the 80,000 volumes in the imposing library, invite guests to private occasions, or simply snooze behind a newspaper in a leather armchair beneath the heavily framed portraits in the Morning Room.

Address 107 Pall Mall, SW1Y 5ER | Getting there Tube to Piccadilly Circus (Bakerloo, Piccadilly Line) | Hours Unless you can get a member to invite you, forget it! | Tip Many clubs prefer not to be identified by a sign on the door. On a walk along Pall Mall, look out for the Travellers Club at 104 Pall Mall; the Reform Club, no. 106; the Army and Navy Club, no. 36; and the Oxford and Cambridge Club, no. 71.

7__ The Barbican

A monstrosity or a home with culture?

It is said that no-one lives in the City, that square mile within London's historic city wall where more than 500,000 people have their place of work and a mere 12,000 their dwelling. One-third of the latter group are at home in The Barbican.

Wartime bombing turned the parish of Cripplegate into an uninhabited field of ruins. In order to breathe life into the City, plans for residential development began in the 1950s, but the project was completed only in the mid-1970s. Some 2,000 flats were constructed from raw-looking, dark concrete, many of them in three towers that rise 123 metres with 42 storeys each. The labyrinth of steps and raised walkways that link the 13 residential blocks can be relied upon to confuse visitors. In keeping with the word 'Barbican', meaning outworks of a fortification, the whole complex turns inwards, saluting its surroundings with concrete cliffs. Is it an urban atrocity?

In fact the Barbican has become a popular, traffic-free place to live and in 2001 received the accolade of a grade-two listing as a site of special architectural interest. The closed-off architecture keeps out the roar of London's streets. Residents are soothed by the sound of splashing fountains on the café terrace and the sight of hanging green gardens or water lilies and reeds in the big pond. The Barbican Arts Centre is a respected venue for cinemas, plays, concerts and exhibitions, and home to a conservatory filled with 2,000 tropical plants. Tourists find historical sights such as the 1,000-year-old church of St Giles-without-Cripplegate. Built in its present form in 1394 and altered many times, it is the church where Oliver Cromwell married and the poet John Milton was laid to rest. Gardens and a moat flank substantial remains of London's medieval city wall with its Roman foundations. As the stone cladding was taken for other purposes, only the core of the wall survives – rough masonry, hardly more attractive than the concrete of the Barbican towers.

Address North of London Wall, EC2Y 8DT, www.barbican.org.uk | **Getting there** Tube to Barbican (Circle, Hammersmith & City, Metropolitan Line) | **Hours** Conservatory visits by appointment, see website for more information | **Tip** South of The Barbican, the historic seat of London's government, Guildhall, stands above the remains of a Roman amphitheatre which, like the hall dating from 1411 and the art gallery, is open to visitors (daily 10am–5pm, Sun noon–4pm).

8_Belgrave Square
Family property

In previous centuries, the art of making the right marriage often determined the prosperity of aristocratic dynasties. In the case of the Grosvenor family, whose head bears the title Duke of Westminster, a well-chosen bride has been effective to this day. The undeveloped land that came to the Grosvenor estates through a 17th-century heiress is now one of the poshest parts of London: Mayfair, Belgravia and Pimlico. The family has kept hold of this prime land, which makes the seventh Duke of Westminster, born in 1991, the richest man of his class.

A centrepiece of this property portfolio is Belgrave Square. At the north-east corner of the square is a memorial to Robert Grosvenor, under whom the neoclassical rows with their columned entrances and white stucco façades were built in the years up to 1840 on marshy terrain that had been a haunt of highwaymen. The duke's architect, George Basevi, designed a row of 11 or 12 imposing houses on each side of the square. In the corners between these terraces he placed palatial detached houses, and the space in the middle was laid out as a garden. Once the home of the aristocracy and the rich, Belgrave Square now serves mainly as a prestigious address for the embassies of Germany, Portugal, Serbia, Bahrain, Norway and Syria. The Duke of Westminster himself has his town house nearby in Eaton Square, which is named after the family's country seat in Cheshire. His London neighbours include Roman Abramovich and Andrew Lloyd Webber.

Fenced in and screened by shrubs from the prying eyes of passers-by, the gardens in the middle of Belgrave Square are a private space. Once a year, however, during the Open Garden Squares Weekend in June, everyone has an opportunity to stroll where otherwise only the privileged residents are admitted. To gain possession of a key to the gate, you need more than a few million pounds.

Address Belgrave Square, SW1X 8PZ | Getting there Tube to Hyde Park Corner
(Piccadilly Line) | Tip In Belgrave Mews behind the German embassy, The Star Tavern
serves excellent Fullers beer and pub food (www.star-tavern-belgravia.co.uk) at prices
that normal people can afford.

9 Berry Bros. & Rudd

Wine merchants for 300 years

The dark green paint on the shop front is the first clue to its age. The windows and doors look as if they have been painted a hundred times without the woodwork ever being sanded down. The surface is covered with little hollows and blisters, and all the corners are rounded, but the paintwork has a deep shine. Inside the shop, oak panelling, dim lighting and the alarming slope of the floor confirm the first impression.

The present building dates from 1731, but a certain Widow Bourne started selling spices, tea and coffee on the site as early as 1698, and soon added wine to her assortment. These origins are dislayed by the sign of a grinder over the door and by huge scales for weighing sacks of coffee beans – and customers too. Regulars can still take advantage of this service and have their names entered in a ledger that records the weight of Lord Byron.

In 1810, George Berry took over the business that now bears the names of his sons and a partner, Hugh Rudd, a specialist in German wines. Today Berry Bros. employ seven qualified 'masters of wine' to advise a discerning clientele, but anyone can walk in and buy a single bottle at an affordable price. The wines on offer range in price from £10 to £10,000. In 2017, the shop moved round the corner to 63 Pall Mall, but the original address is still the company headquarters.

The longevity of this wine merchant is connected to its prime location in St James's, where the well-to-do gentleman has his essential suppliers. Opposite Berry Bros., Truefitt & Hill sell exquisite shaving accessories. The hat maker Locke, the shoe maker Lobb and Dunhill's cigar shop are close by, and fine shirts can be purchased round the corner in Jermyn Street. For all its air of tradition, Berry Bros. has large modern storehouses outside London and sells online – but to buy their wine in style, only one place will do.

Address 3 St James's Street, SW1A 1EG, www.bbr.com | Getting there Tube to Green Park (Piccadilly, Victoria Line) | Hours Tue–Sat 10am–5pm | Tip The Red Lion in Crown Passage between King Street and Pall Mall is a historic pub with lots of atmosphere.

10 Bevis Marks Synagogue

A 300-year-old Jewish community

London's oldest synagogue lies hidden between office blocks. Its inconspicuousness is not only the result of incessant construction work in the City: when it was founded, Jewish places of worship were not allowed to stand directly on a public thoroughfare. In view of the roaring traffic all around, the sheltered location in a courtyard off the street Bevis Marks is a blessing today both for the congregation and for visitors who come to enjoy a historic and architectural jewel.

After a period of 350 years during which it was prohibited to practise the Jewish religion in England, in 1656 Jews who had been expelled from Spain and Portugal, and had worshipped in London discreetly for several years, established a small synagogue in Creechurch Lane near Bevis Marks. Their community flourished and commissioned Joseph Avis, a pupil of Sir Christopher Wren, to build a new synagogue, which was opened in 1701 and has hardly been changed since then.

The most striking features inside are the raised reading desk and the ark, a decorated cupboard on the east wall to hold the torah. The ark is made of painted oak with Corinthian columns and beautiful woodcarving. Seven many-branched chandeliers stand for the days of the week, and the twelve columns supporting the women's gallery symbolise the tribes of Israel. The plain benches at the back are survivals from the old building in Creechurch Lane; the reason why the others are so uncomfortable is said to be that Avis was a Puritan.

In the 19th century the synagogue was almost closed, as the long-established Jewish community had moved out of the City, and poor Jewish immigrants were living further east. Today, services are held early in the morning on weekdays for employees of the surrounding banks. Judaism has been practised in Bevis Marks Synagogue without interruption for over 300 years, making it unique in all of Europe.

קדש לה
ק ק
שער השמים
רה התסב

A.M.
5461.
1701.

Address Bevis Marks, E1 7AA, www.sephardi.org.uk/bevis-marks | Getting there Tube to Aldgate (Central, Metropolitan Line) | Hours Mon, Wed, Thu 10.30am–2pm, Tue & Fri 10.30am–1pm, Sun 10.30am–12.30pm | Tip The Jewish Museum in Camden (129 Albert Street, Sun–Thu 10am–5pm, Fri 10am–2pm) presents Jewish culture and the history of Judaism in Britain.

11 The Boat Gardens

Pink blossom on the grey river

A short walk downstream from Tower Bridge, a stroll on the south bank of the river reveals a surprising sight: trees and gardens on the River Thames. Here, at Tower Bridge Moorings, old barges rock gently on the waves. Thirty historic boats have been tied together, seven of them forming a long green corridor.

The idea for a river garden came to the architect Nick Lacey in the 1990s. The first barge to be planted was called *Silo*. It was beautified with box hedges, honeysuckle and a weeping alder. Soon lilac, birches, pear trees, clematis and climbing jasmine were flourishing on the other boats. From the early-flowering cherry in winter, the show of blossom and colour continues through the year until berries and foliage glow in autumn. Evergreens such as holly and holm oak are present too. Tiny informal gardens on boat roofs are a common sight on London's waterways, but these barges have been laid out according to an overall plan: a row of medlars upriver is mirrored at the eastern end by a miniature avenue of quince. Herbs, grasses, ferns and a myriad flowers – iris, vetch, nasturtiums and more – grow in steel tubs 30 centimetres deep beneath the trees and shrubs.

With the help of the residents, two gardeners apply organic methods of work to attract as many birds, bees and other pollinating insects as possible. Although blue tits, goldfinches and chiff-chaffs are regular visitors, snails have too few natural predators here and are removed by hand. Sometimes geese and coots hatch their eggs on the water next to the barges. Some 70 residents of a floating community have access to their homes via the gardens. This creative village successfully resisted the local authority, which wanted to close it in 2004. Today the garden barges are no longer under threat, and have even won the gold award of the Borough of Southwark for the best community garden.

Address Bermondsey Wall West | Getting there Tube to Bermondsey (Jubilee Line), or walk east from Tower Bridge | Hours Open to the public only on special occasions: see www.ngs.org.uk or www.opensquares.org | Tip Next to the moorings, the little River Neckinger flows into the Thames. Historic warehouses now converted into flats that line its banks in Mill Street and Shad Thames make this an interesting place for a walk.

12 Brixton Market

An explosion of colours and flavours

Brixton has had its ups and downs. In the late 19th century it was a prosperous district. It then became a working-class area, and after the Second World War had an Afro-Caribbean population. The first Jamaicans came straight from their ship to temporary accommodation in a bomb shelter in 1948, and the nearest job exchange was in Brixton, which today is a mixed quarter with immigrants from different continents, including Africa and South America. At times Brixton has had a reputation for drug-related crime. These issues have not disappeared, but in recent years the district has shown its strengths, including a creative cultural scene and vibrant markets.

Parading Rastafarian dreadlocks, headscarves and African or Asian robes, the traders and their customers are visibly part of a multicultural quarter. The products are equally diverse: yams, plantains and manioc, dried fish from West Africa, religious items from Haiti, Chinese herbs, huge cooking pots, metal bins filled with brooms and mops. On Brixton Road lies the art deco entrance to Reliance Arcade, a narrow passageway filled from end to end with tiny hairdressers' salons, where women have their hair elaborately plaited and styled. At the end of this arcade you cross Electric Lane to reach Market Row, and beyond this is the brightly painted Brixton Village market hall. Here salsa music booms out from a Columbian butcher's stand, while other stalls rock to the sounds of reggae and soul.

Gentrification has begun: shops selling designer items and vintage fashion have moved in, and trendy world-cuisine eateries have opened, offering sourdough pizza and gourmet burgers, but also down-to-earth meals of Jamaican curry and Chinese dumplings. The adjacent Electric Avenue, too, is a colourful market street, where Rasta-look clothes in bright colours bearing the face of Bob Marley are on sale.

Address Electric Avenue, SW9 8JX, www.brixtonmarket.net | Getting there Overground or Victoria Line to Brixton | Hours Open daily; for more info visit website | Tip On the other side of the railway arches, via Pope's Road, is Pop Brixton – a cool container-built village for creative start-ups, market stalls, street food, cocktails and live music (Sun–Wed 9am–11pm, Thu–Sat 9am–midnight).

13 Brockwell Park

Adele was moved to tears

Between the districts of Brixton, Herne Hill and Tulse Hill, a green space of 120 acres breaks up the endless rows of houses in south London, and provides many kinds of recreation for local residents. The singer Adele grew up in this area, and once explained why she didn't go to summer festivals: 'I preferred to sit in Brockwell Park with my friends and drink cider.' In fact, the park was often a venue for festivals, at which artists such as Elvis Costello and Grace Jones performed.

Plenty of entertainment is on offer even when no events are taking place. Hilltop grassy spaces give a panoramic view of the central London skyline. Swans glide across the ponds in the western part of the park, while on its eastern edge humans take to the water in Brockwell Lido, a heritage-listed, renovated pool dating from the 1930s. Art lovers can admire sculptures, while for kids there are playgrounds, a miniature railway and a BMX halfpipe. Near the highest point of the park stands Brockwell Hall, built 200 years ago as a country house for a merchant. In 1891, London County Council bought the estate and opened it to the public. Today, Brockwell Hall houses a café. Nearby is a walled garden where shrubs and plants of all kinds, sheltered from the winds, produce a show of colour even early in the year.

In late July, rustic life visits south London when Lambeth Country Show is held in Brockwell Park. The animals from Vauxhall City Farm are on show, sheep-shearing contests take place, and the growers of vegetables, fruit and flowers compete for gold medals. A lot of music is performed, of course, from reggae to ska and samba. Perhaps Adele will even take to the stage one day. Explaining the lyrics of her song 'Million Years Ago', which looks back wistfully to her carefree years in this area before she became famous, Adele said: 'I drove past Brockwell Park … and burst into tears.'

Address Norwood Road, SE24 9BJ | **Getting there** Train to Herne Hill, 10 minutes from Victoria, 12 minutes from Blackfriars; walk from Brixton (see ch. 12), about half a mile south of Brixton Station, via Brixton Road/Effra Road, then left into Brixton Water Lane | **Hours** Daily 7.30am until 15 minutes before dusk | **Tip** Next to Herne Hill Station, traffic-calmed Railton Road has a nice mix of cafés and small shops, as well as a Sunday market (11am–4pm) with crafts and street food.

14 The Brunswick Plane

The urban tree

London's characteristic tree is the plane. It adorns many streets with broad leaves and bark that varies in colour from grey and brown to green and mauve. It shades office workers during their midday break, nourishes squirrels with its seeds, and after the leaves have fallen, the plane's attractive spherical fruit remains hanging for months more. One of the most magnificent examples of the species, the 'Brunswick plane', stands on the lawn in Brunswick Square. Its circumference measures seven metres. Because, unusually, its lower branches were not cut off, this specimen spreads out at head height. At the centre of a wide expanse of grass, the tree had the freedom to grow in its splendid natural shape.

The London plane (Platanus x acerifolia) is a separate species, probably a cross of the oriental plane (P. orientalis) and the American sycamore (P. occidentalis). In cities it attains a height of 30 to 35 metres, in the country 45 metres or more in exceptional cases. Its suitability as an urban tree was recognised in the 18th century. It is resistant against frost, drought, waterlogged conditions, compacted soil and – most important of all in the days of London smog – against pollution. Toxins cannot easily penetrate the tree, as its bark flakes off in patches and rain washes its hard, shiny leaves. It is not known how long a London plane can live, as none are thought to have died of old age. Some are 350 years old.

The tree on Brunswick Square, which has outlasted the original surrounding buildings, was probably planted between 1795 and 1802, a time when this part of Bloomsbury was a fine address: in Jane Austen's Emma, Mr and Mrs Knightley live on Brunswick Square. It is included on the list of 'Great Trees of London' along with many other planes, notably the Victorian specimen on Berkeley Square, one among many fine examples on that square, and a famous tree by the entrance to the Dorchester Hotel.

Address Brunswick Square, WC1N 1AZ | Getting there Tube to Russell Square
(Piccadilly Line) | Tip The Foundling Museum at the north-east corner of Brunswick
Square has an exquisite art collection, including works by Hogarth and Gainsborough
(Tue–Sat 10am–5pm, Sun 11am–5pm, www.foundlingmuseum.org.uk).

15 — Bunhill Fields

Lunch among the tombstones

Green spaces are precious in the City. Office workers who cannot face the idea of eating with their colleagues in the canteen yet again buy a sandwich or a salad and take it to a bench in a nearby park. And if the park happens to be a cemetery, as in the case of Bunhill Fields on the northern edge of the finance district, why should that spoil their appetite?

The name derives from 'bone hill'. In the 16th century, human remains were piled up here on marshy ground and covered with earth, as the ossuary of St Paul's Cathedral was full to the brim. After the Great Plague of 1665, thousands more bodies were dumped on the site, which then remained in use as an unconsecrated burial ground – not for Anglicans but for Dissenters, i.e. members of the Baptist, Quaker and other Protestant groups. By the time the cemetery was closed in 1852, tens of thousands had been laid to rest here, including some prominent persons: Daniel Defoe, the author of Robinson Crusoe; the itinerant preacher John Bunyan, who wrote The Pilgrim's Progress; and the visionary poet and artist William Blake.

In the 19th century, and again in the 1960s following war damage, Bunhill Fields was made into a park. Mossy stones, crosses leaning at an angle and a few massive, ivy-covered tombs stand in densely packed rows beneath plane, oak, ash and sycamore trees. Defoe is honoured by an obelisk, Bunyan by a large tomb bearing the image of a pilgrim. Perhaps the most edifying grave of all is that of Mary Page, with an inscription detailing the sufferings that she endured with Christian fortitude: she had so much fluid in her body that it had to be tapped 66 times in the space of 67 months, extracting no less than 240 gallons altogether. Relaxing on seats with a view of this medical history, office workers from the City wash down their ciabatta and baguette with gallons of caffè latte.

Address Between City Road and Bunhill Row, EC1Y 2BG | Getting there Tube to Old Street (Northern Line) | Hours Mon–Fri 8am–7pm, Sat & Sun 9.30am–7pm or until dusk | Tip Directly opposite Bunhill Fields on City Road are the chapel and house of John Wesley (1703–1791), the founder of Methodism. A museum there is devoted to the history of this denomination (for opening hours see www.wesleysheritage.org.uk).

16 Bushy Park

The beginning of a mass movement

The bronze statue of the goddess Diana at the centre of a pond was made for a queen, and now watches over a weekly event that improved the lives of many of the Queen's subjects. In 1637, Charles I commissioned the figure as a present for his consort, Henrietta Maria. 70 years later it was removed from Hampton Court Palace and placed a few hundred metres away in Bushy Park, where it is an eye-catcher at the junction of an avenue of chestnuts with an avenue of lime trees. Every Saturday, several hundred people gather here for their weekly parkrun.

This event began in 2004, when Paul Sinton-Hewitt, a dedicated runner, was injured and unable to take his favourite form of exercise. To snap out of his feelings of depression, he organised a five-kilometre run for friends in Bushy Park and recorded their times. Thirteen people took part, with three volunteers to show the way. The idea took off and spread to other parks. Fifteen years after the first event, almost 2,000 weekly parkruns – non-commercial and free of charge for everyone – were being held in more than 20 countries, and 4 million people had sprinted, jogged or walked their local course to reach a total combined distance of 250 million kilometres.

It is, of course, possible to enjoy the 1,100-acre park without pulling on the running shoes. Herds of red and fallow deer roam the grassy open spaces. The baroque Upper Lodge Water Garden in the north-west has ponds and cascades, and the Waterhouse Woodland Garden to the north of the fountain of Diana is a pleasant place to stroll beneath willows and birch trees. Near Shaef Gate in the north-east, a memorial marks the site of General Eisenhower's tent in Camp Griffiss, where he planned the D-Day invasion of Normandy. For refreshments, stop afterwards at the Pheasantry Café, where park runners meet on Saturdays after their event.

Address Hampton Court Road, KT8 9DD (entrance), www.royalparks.org.uk; see also www.parkrun.com | **Getting there** Train from Waterloo to Hampton Court, then a 10-minute walk across the Thames and past Hampton Court Palace | **Hours** Park open at all times; Water Gardens, Woodlands Gardens: daily 9am–dusk (Water Gardens closed Mon); Pheasantry Café: Mar–Oct 9am–6pm, winter 9am–5pm | **Tip** From the fountain of Diana, the chestnut avenue leads to the Lion Gate of Hampton Court, where admission is free to the flower gardens and Tiltyard Café.

17 Cabbies' Shelter in Grosvenor Gardens

Huts that are architectural heritage

London taxis are famous around the world, of course. Some 21,000 'black cabs' – the name sticks despite their modern appearance in all sorts of garish colours – operate on the city's streets. Less well known and much less numerous are the green-painted wooden huts that were built in the late 19th century as places of rest and refreshment for the drivers of hansom cabs. Thirteen of them are still standing, every one a listed structure and thus protected from demolition. Some 150 years ago, the drivers of two-wheeled hansom cabs were not allowed to leave their vehicles during a shift, and therefore seldom got a warm meal although they were out in all weathers. A charity called the Cabmen's Shelter Fund took pity on them and built 61 huts at cab ranks between 1875 and 1914. As they stood on public highways, the shelters were not allowed to occupy a surface larger than a horse and carriage, but each of them was fitted with a small kitchen and seating for 10 to 12 persons. Alcohol and gambling were banned – the approved pastime was to read mind-improving literature donated by publishers.

Some cabbies' shelters, like that in Grosvenor Gardens and those on Hanover Square, next to Temple Tube station and in Thurloe Place opposite the Victoria and Albert Museum, still serve tea, coffee, sandwiches and light meals to taxi drivers. Others, such as the hut near Embankment station, are deserted, no more than lifeless monuments to days that have passed. Despite the modest size of the shelters, they have architectural dignity thanks to a harmonious composition of windows, panels and perforated decoration in the shape of plant motifs. Small triangles like pediments provide ventilation, a chimney surmounts the roof of wooden shingles, and overhanging eaves protect customers when they buy their tea. It is a simple and attractive design.

Address Grosvenor Gardens, west side, SW1W | **Getting there** Tube to Victoria (Circle, District, Victoria Line) | **Tip** The bronze sculpture of a lion hunting a kudu antelope in Upper Grosvenor Gardens was made by Jonathan Kenworthy and commissioned by Gerald Grosvenor, sixth Duke of Westminster.

18 Chinatown

An enclave in Soho

Immigrant communities have put their stamp on a number of different districts in London. These are usually poor areas outside the city centre. South Lambeth Road is Little Portugal, Edgware Road has a marked Arab character and, way out west, Southall has a large Punjabi population. Thanks to its location in the West End, Chinatown is different. A small area around Gerrard Street and Lisle Street is home to 80 Chinese restaurants. Red-painted Chinese arches with green-glazed roof tiles greet crowds of visitors, two pop-eyed stone lions glower up Macclesfield Street, crispy brown Peking duck hangs in the windows, and streets are named in Chinese characters. Chinatown is a colourful, bustling tourist attraction – but is it authentic?

In the 18th century, sailors from the Far East lived in dockland areas such as Limehouse, which was known for its Chinese laundries 100 years ago. Bombing in the Second World War scattered this community, but a regrouping took place after the war thanks to the return of British soldiers. Some of them had acquired a taste for Asian food. The first Chinese restaurants opened in seedy Soho, where rents were low. As Cantonese immigrants arrived from Hong Kong, the area slowly acquired its character, which is more than a row of eateries for visitors. Chinese really do live here, working in supermarkets, bakeries, herbalists and medicinal practices as well as restaurants. They have their own lawyers, travel agents and accountants. In Charing Cross Road, the Westminster Chinese Library was established, in Leicester Court the Chinese Community Centre.

Paradoxically, apart from this single high concentration around Gerrard Street, London's estimated 100,000 residents of Chinese origin are thinly spread across the city. The reason may be that many of them still run restaurants, which prosper in the suburbs by keeping a distance from their rivals.

Address Between Shaftesbury Avenue and Leicester Square, W1D 5PJ | Getting there Tube to Leicester Square (Northern, Piccadilly Line) | Tip The Oversea Chinese Restaurant serves excellent dim sum (7 Gerrard Street, daily noon – midnight).

19_Christie's

Classier than eBay

London's art scene comprises world-class museums with famous paintings and cutting-edge East End galleries, famous artists and anonymous but talented sprayers. Three long-established auction houses belong to the conventional end of this spectrum: Sotheby's in Bond Street, Bonham's in New Bond Street – and Christie's, founded in 1760 and domiciled in King Street in the St James's district since 1823.

Is the National Gallery too crowded, and the latest special exhibition at the British Museum too expensive? For a quieter alternative that is free of charge, it is worth paying a visit to an auction house where paintings, exquisite furniture, sculptures, objets d'art and everything else that rich collectors covet are on display. The viewing dates can be seen on the auction houses' internet sites. Anyone can walk in and look around. Discreet, polite, well-informed members of staff may approach with advice or information, but no-one need fear being put under pressure or made to feel embarrassed about their ignorance. Most people, however, will be more at ease if they are well-dressed when they enter the well-appointed premises. So don't be shy, just walk inside and ascend the stairs that lead to three museum- like galleries. Beyond them lies the auction room with its rows of seats and auctioneer's desk.

Christie's employs experts for every imaginable field: old masters and contemporary painting, art from Africa and Oceania, jewellery, silver, carpets, cigars and wine. Trustworthy guests may pick up or touch items that would be locked behind glass in the Victoria and Albert Museum. If the exhibits do not appeal, it is entertaining to watch the other visitors: distinguished older men, elegant ladies, girls in jeans who seem to be in their teens but might be billionaires' daughters. Which of them will be bidding in the auction tomorrow?

Address 8 King Street, SW1Y 6QT, www.christies.com | Getting there Tube to Green Park (Jubilee, Piccadilly, Victoria Line) | Hours Mon–Fri 9.30am–4.30pm | Tip For people who can afford to buy art at Christie's, The Wolseley (160 Piccadilly, daily 8am–midnight) is the place to eat.

20 City Hall

A skewed seat of government

What a location! City Hall lies on the south bank of the Thames next to Tower Bridge, with a fine view across the river to the Tower of London and the skyscrapers of the financial district. When building a new seat of government for one of the world's greatest cities on a site like this, architecture of high calibre was called for. The result, a 10-storey modified sphere with a pronounced lean, met with acclaim from some quarters, but has also been described as a misshapen egg, Darth Vader's helmet, and a glass testicle.

Why did London get a new City Hall in 2002? Opposite it on the north bank is the historic City of London, the 'square mile', now mainly a banking district. This precinct has its own ancient seat of government, Guildhall, and a lord mayor with ceremonial duties. City Hall by contrast is the headquarters of the Greater London Authority, which administers the whole metropolitan area. It is run by the Mayor of London and London Assembly. Because the left-wing Greater London Council was a thorn in Margaret Thatcher's flesh in the 1980s, she dissolved it. The city had no overall administration until the Labour government instituted the first directly elected mayor for all of London in 2000.

This called for a new seat of government, City Hall, designed by the renowned architects Foster and Partners. They used a lot of glass to symbolise open government. A 500-metre spiral ramp from the basement to the top floor surrounds the assembly chamber and affords views inside, making speakers feel like goldfish in a giant bowl. Visitors can walk up it as far as the second floor. The most striking aspect of the building, its 31-degree southward tilt, makes it energy-efficient. On the lower storey, where the floor covering is a satellite image of London, the café is open to everybody. City Hall is a metaphor for London itself: surprising, provocative, lovably out of kilter.

Address The Queen's Walk, SE1 2AA | Getting there Tube to London Bridge (Jubilee, Northern Line) | Hours Mon–Thu 8.30am–6pm, Fri 8.30am–5.30pm | Tip A few minutes' walk west along the river bank is Hay's Galleria, a warehouse with wharf that has been converted to an atrium of restaurants and shops.

21 The Coade Stone Lion
Unexpectedly humble origins

The eastern approach to Westminster Bridge is guarded by a majestic stone lion with a luxuriant mane. From its granite plinth on the north parapet of the bridge, it watches over those who cross the Thames towards Parliament. It might be thought a worthy symbol of power from the days when London was the capital of a global empire – but in fact this is a brewery lion, and is not even made of real stone.

The material is 'Coade stone', a ceramic product that was made in the factory of Mrs Eleanor Coade in Lambeth between 1770 and the 1840s. The recipe was 60 per cent clay with additions of ground glass, flint and a little quartz. Coade stone was extremely resistant to weathering and corrosion caused by soot, important properties in smoggy 19th-century London. The mixture was shaped in moulds to make unique items or low-cost mass products, and was fired four days long at a high, constant temperature. This technical achievement, and the fact that standard parts could be combined in varied ways for individual designs, made Coade stone popular for monuments and architectural adornment. Further examples of its use are the figures above the entrance of Twinings tea shop on The Strand, the tomb of Captain Bligh (of the mutiny on the Bounty) in the churchyard of St Mary's Lambeth, sculptures above the entrance to the Imperial War Museum and architectural details in the chapel of the Old Naval College in Greenwich.

In 1837, the sculptor William Woodington made two lions to stand on top of the Red Lion Brewery on the south bank of the Thames. When the brewery was demolished in 1950 and the Festival of Britain was held on its site, the red paint was stripped from one lion and, at the wish of King George VI, the figure was placed in front of Waterloo Station. It came to the bridge in 1966. The second lion, shining gold, growls down at visitors from the gate of Twickenham rugby stadium.

Address Westminster Bridge Road, SE1 7PB | Getting there Tube to Westminster (Circle, District, Jubilee Line) | Tip One legacy of the Festival of Britain is an example of good 1950s' architecture: the Royal Festival Hall, with the upmarket bar-restaurant Skylon and a view of the river from the café.

22 Cousin Lane Stairs

Down to a beach on the Thames

In centuries past, when rowing boats carried passengers along the river, many flights of steps were needed to give access to landing stages. In the heart of the city few such stairs have survived, one of them at the end of Cousin Lane. Here you can descend to a hidden beach at ebb tide (but take care, as the steps can be slippery), in order to see, hear and smell London from an unfamiliar angle.

Down on the shore, the noise of road traffic recedes, but trains rumble across Cannon Street Bridge, and the waves from Thames Clippers splash up on the little beach. Pebbles crunch beneath your feet. Looking down, you see stones of many colours, pieces of brick rounded by the river current, shards of pottery, animal bones and oyster shells, and at low water, you can walk across this uneven ground for about 100 metres in both directions for a water-snail's view of bridges and embankments.

This is not the prosperous, shiny surface of London, but its many-layered underside. The high quayside walls, full of holes and patched up in brick, are covered in green slime and fronds. Heavy chains hang from them, and rotting timbers rise from the river bed. A round iron gate in the wall and a concrete channel for its outflow are reminders of the dank warren of sewers and underground streams that lies beneath the streets. The Walbrook, which flowed through the Roman and medieval city, reached the Thames close to this spot. On beaches like this, the tides and river current scour the river bed and bring London's past to light. In the late 1950s, a 14th-century sword was turned up close by. Broken clay pipes and coins are found all the time by Thames mudlarks, whose hobby is digging up history in the Thames.

The atmosphere of Cousin Lane Stairs has been captured at www.soundsurvey.org.uk, an acoustic map of the city: click on Sound Maps, square no. 58, then scroll down in the box.

Address Between Thames Street and the river, immediately west of Cannon Street Station, EC4R 3TE | Getting there Tube to Cannon Street (Circle, District Line) | Tip Next to Cousin Lane Stairs, Steelyard Passage leads beneath the railway bridge. From the 13th century, the Steelyard was the London depot of the Hanseatic League of German trading cities. A plaque on the east side of the bridge commemorates it.

23__ Cross Bones Graveyard

In memory of the outcast and downtrodden

A patch of wasteland behind a high wall in a run-down corner of Southwark has become a shrine and a place of popular protest. Passers-by can see little through the locked metal gates, as they are covered from top to bottom with colourful strips of cloth, plastic flowers, scraps of paper inscribed with prayers, poems, and hand-written messages to deceased relatives, Christmas tree decorations, teddy bears and crocheted dolls, dream catchers, images of Indian goddesses, small mirrors, chestnuts threaded on string. Many people have expressed their wishes and emotions here through words and objects. A Madonna hangs from the gate, but this is no Christian sanctuary – in fact, it was an unconsecrated graveyard.

Until the 17th century, prostitutes, known as 'Winchester geese', were buried here within the jurisdiction of the bishops of Winchester. Beyond the control of the City of London authorities, the see of Winchester licensed brothels, arenas for bull baiting, and theatres. The bishops profited from this business, but gave no Christian burial to 'dishonoured' women. Crossbones later became a Christian cemetery for the poor and was closed in 1852, when an estimated 15,000 graves had filled it to overflowing. In the 1990s, archaeologists who examined 148 skeletons from the site found one-third of them to be new-born or still-born children.

Although this unbuilt site is a mouth-watering prospect for developers, an alliance of residents, mystics, feminists and the local writer John Constable, whose Southwark Mysteries were inspired, he claims, by the spirit of a Winchester goose, have persuaded the landowner, Transport for London, to lease the site to the Bankside Open Spaces Trust, which has preserved the remains of the dead and is creating a garden with volunteer workers and wardens. A wildlife meadow, pond and the Goosewing Entrance made by the woodworker Arthur DeMowbray can be visited.

Address Redcross Way, SE1 1TA | Getting there Tube to Borough (Northern Line) | Hours Normally Wed–Fri noon–2pm, see www.bost.org.uk | Tip On the Thames path close to Southwark Cathedral stands a high wall with a rose window – remains of the magnificent palace of the bishops of Winchester, which stood here from the 12th to the 17th century.

24 The Duke of York Column

A man who made it to the top

The famous column is of course the one dedicated to Horatio Nelson on Trafalgar Square, but the admiral does not stand as high as a much less glorious contemporary: Frederick, Duke of York. The second son of King George III, his early life was nothing unusual for a prince of German lineage. In 1764, at the age of six months, he was made Prince Bishop of Osnabrück. He later married a daughter of Frederick William II of Prussia.

So far, so good – but then he embarked on a military career, commanding British forces in Flanders against the French revolutionary armies in 1793. After initial successes, he retreated to Hanover, the historic family seat, and sailed home in 1795 without having accomplished much. His father rewarded these exploits by making the Duke of York a field marshal and commander-in-chief of the army. In 1799 his expedition to the Netherlands was so calamitous that he was forced to withdraw after three months. The campaign gave rise to the children's rhyme: 'The Grand Old Duke of York, he had ten thousand men, he marched them up to the top of the hill and he marched them down again.'

Back in England, things scarcely improved. His mistress felt obliged to cover household expenses by selling officers' patents, as her royal lover had squandered huge sums on horses. The ensuing scandal forced the Duke to resign his command. He has nevertheless earned praise from army historians for his reforms, which are held to have paved the way for later military successes. After his death in 1827, one day's wages was withheld from every British soldier in order to finance the monument. The Duke of York looks down on St James's Park from a 42-metre granite column. The viewing platform, once a favourite place for suicide, is no longer open to the public. The statue is said to have been placed so high in order to keep the Duke out of reach of his creditors.

Address Waterloo Place, SW1Y 5AH | Getting there Tube to Charing Cross (Bakerloo, Northern Line) | Tip Behind a gate next to the column is the tombstone of Giro, the German ambassador's terrier, who died in 1934 when he gnawed through an electric cable.

25 East India Dock

Spice and dragonflies

Poplar in east London was once one of the British Empire's most important trading centres. Ships of the East India Company, founded in 1600, set out from the Thames for South Asia and China, returning with luxury goods such as tea, spices, silk and carpets. In 1803, the East India Company began constructing docks large enough for 1,400-tonne vessels over 50 metres long – an enormous undertaking, as thousands of tonnes of earth and mud had to be excavated by the muscle-power of humans and horses.

After the closure of these docks in 1967, two sections were filled in. The site of the Export Dock to the west is now occupied by housing. All that remains of the Import Dock, north of the elevated rail tracks, is an ornamental patch of open water, and street names that hark back to the old trading days: Saffron Avenue, Clove Crescent, Nutmeg Lane.

The East India Dock Basin that survives today was merely the entrance to the larger harbour beyond. It's now a nature reserve. Brackish water flows in from the Thames, bringing fish, eels and small crustaceans that serve as a larder for gulls and kingfishers. Ducks and swans feed in reed beds and patches of muddy salt marsh. Flowering plants in and around the water attract butterflies. Spring sees the arrival of common terns, which raise their young here in May and June on specially built nesting rafts, departing for Africa when summer ends. Dragonflies hunt smaller insects among the dense reeds. The black redstart, a rare bird in Britain, nests in holes and crevices.

The lock gates are impressive structures dating from 1879. Next to them, Roman numerals cut into the stone quayside mark the water level. There's also a sweeping view across the river to the O2 Dome in North Greenwich, westwards to the towers of Canary Wharf, and eastwards towards the estuary, from where the East Indiamen once sailed with their precious cargo.

Address Blackwall Way, E14 9QS | Getting there DLR to East India, then a five-minute walk east along Blackwall Way | Hours Daily 8am–7.30pm | Tip The eastern exit from the dock leads via Orchard Place to Trinity Buoy Wharf, with its imaginative public art, a container village for creative start-ups, and Fatboy's Diner.

26__Eccleston Mews
Ideal homes in the stables

A 'mews', a small service road for stables, deliveries and servants at the back of the fine houses of the rich, is a London phenomenon. They are common in districts such as Kensington, Mayfair and Bayswater, and almost unknown outside London. Eccleston Mews, built in the 19th century in Belgravia, is one example of many quiet enclaves that can be seen on a walk around London.

When residences for high society with imposing classical architecture were built in terraces around the broad streets and garden squares of Belgravia, it was out of the question that stables or tradesmen's entrances would spoil the view of the façade. The solution was to place a humble street at the back, sometimes semi-concealed behind an archway. Here horses and carriages were accommodated on the ground floor of plain buildings, while grooms and servants could live on the upper floor. In the 20th century, the motor car made these stables obsolete, and ever fewer families could afford a mansion with a large staff of servants. Little by little, mews buildings were converted to garages or dwellings. From the 1950s they came into vogue as affordable, discreet addresses in top locations for creative people. The painter Francis Bacon was among the first artists to inhabit a mews. In the Swinging Sixties, to live in a mews was considered unconventional and slightly racy. In the film A Hard Day's Night, the Beatles occupied a mews flat, as did John Steed, the hero of the TV series The Avengers.

Apart from the Royal Mews at Buckingham Palace, only one has remained in uninterrupted operation as a stable: Bathurst Mews to the north of Hyde Park is still home to a riding school. Mews houses, enlarged by cellar and attic conversions, are now sold at dizzying prices. Often a Bentley or Jaguar is parked outside, but the street name reveals that these were once homes for horses and servants.

Address Between Eaton Square and Eaton Place, SW1W 9AD | **Getting there** Tube to Victoria (Circle, District, Victoria Line) | **Tip** In the Royal Mews at Buckingham Palace, the Queen's collection of coaches and limousines is on display (for opening times see www.rct.uk).

27 — The Ecuadorean Embassy

Asylum for Julian Assange

For seven years the corner balcony of the Ecuadorean Embassy held the attention of global media. On 19 June, 2012, the Australian activist Julian Assange, founder of Wikileaks, was granted asylum in the embassy. A British court had ordered his extradition to Sweden on charges of rape. However, Assange feared that Sweden would deport him to face a long prison sentence in the USA for revealing secrets about the Iraq War. He jumped bail and was taken in by Ecuador, as that country was in dispute with Washington at the time.

Until 2019 he shared the eight rooms of the embassy with the South American diplomats. From time to time Assange appeared on the balcony and spoke to the media or raised a defiant fist to gatherings of sympathisers. He received well-known visitors, including Lady Gaga, the actor Pamela Anderson and politician Nigel Farage. The reporters waiting outside usually had to content themselves with glimpses of Assange's cat in the window. Wearing a collar and a colourful array of miniature neckties, it stared longingly at the outside world. Assange and his partner had two children during the asylum years, but this did not become known until 2020.

The task of guarding the embassy cost the British state £12 million, and Ecuador is said to have spent millions on security measures, board and lodgings for Assange. Three ambassadors came and went during his stay, which ended acrimoniously. Assange was accused by his hosts of spying on them, insulting embassy staff and leading an unhygienic lifestyle. Counter-accusations were made about espionage against Assange. In April 2019, visibly aged and in poor health, he was handed over to the police, who had to drag their protesting prisoner into a van. He was jailed for 50 weeks for breaching his conditions of bail. In 2021, a judge refused extradition to the USA on grounds of mental health, but at the time of writing Assange remains in prison while an appeal is considered.

Address 3 Hans Crescent, SW1X 0LN | **Getting there** Tube to Knightsbridge (Piccadilly Line) | **Tip** Although Harrods is a tourist trap, a visit to the wonderful food halls is worthwhile – for the architecture, or for fine picnic ingredients to eat in Hyde Park.

28__Edgware Road
'Little Beirut' in London

London, where a third of the population was born abroad, is probably more multicultural than any city in the world apart from New York. The faces, clothing and languages spoken make it obvious that dozens of different ethnic groups live here. Some concentrate in a particular area – east Africans in North Kensington, for example, Turks in Dalston. European and English-speaking immigrants also have their favourite quarters. Five per cent of the residents in Chelsea are US citizens, and a Cypriot community has congregated in Camberwell. Lovers of Portuguese food head for South Lambeth Road, and those who like Arab cooking are spoiled for choice on Edgware Road.

At its southern end near Marble Arch, expensive Lebanese restaurants put on live music and belly-dancing. Further out, north of Edgware Road Tube station, a simpler style takes over. Syrians and Iraqis run grocery stores and eateries with plain furnishings that serve delicious meals for a low price. Newsagents sell Arabic newspapers, fashion outlets cater for ladies who prefer to reveal little, and numerous TV screens show the latest football match from Egypt or the news from Al Jazeera channel. When the weather is fine, cafés in Praed Street put shisha pipes out on the pavement.

Arabs trading with the Ottoman Empire settled in this area 100 years ago. In the 1950s, many Egyptians arrived, and since then every crisis in the Middle East has brought more immigrants. Lebanese and Palestinians fled from war, Algerians from violent civil unrest, Syrians and Iraqis from recent horrors in their region. While rich Arabs in search of sound investments and desirable residences have bought property in Knightsbridge – although the Egyptian Mohamed al-Fayed no longer owns Harrods – and Mayfair, to enjoy some Arab atmosphere, avoid these haunts of the super-rich and walk across Hyde Park to Edgware Road.

Address Edgware Road, W2 2HZ: walk north-west from Marble Arch | Getting there Tube to Edgware Road (Circle, District Line) | Tip Go to the canal basin between Edgware Road and Paddington Station to see Thomas Heatherwick's Rolling Bridge, which opens hydraulically by rolling up, as demonstrated every Wednesday and Friday at noon.

29 Eel Pie Island

A refuge for artists and musicians

This island in the Thames takes its name from the fare that was served in inns in the 18th and 19th centuries, when guests came by boat for dances. Today, a narrow pedestrian bridge leads to tranquillity and seclusion in leafy surroundings rather than pies and dance music. There are no cars on the island, not even bicycles – just a path leading to Richmond Yacht Club, Twickenham Rowing Club and 50 houses, whose occupants clearly value their peace and quiet, as signs politely point out that the gardens are private property. On two weekends in summer, when 20 or more artists, including painters, sculptors, potters and glass artists, open their studios, visitors are allowed to see more. In a yard on the north bank, ship's carpenters, welders and metalworkers repair and build boats. Sedate cabin cruisers and sleek motor yachts bob up and down by the quay and in boat-houses. The two tips of the 700-metre-long island are nature reserves.

The island has not always been a mix of residential idyll and place of work. In the 1950s, the run-down Eel Pie Hotel, known in the pre-war years for its genteel tea dances, was a venue for hot new music and one of the best places for British jazz.

Rhythm 'n' blues and rock were the thing in the early 1960s. Rod Stewart, The Who, Pink Floyd and The Rolling Stones all played on Eel Pie Island before they became famous. The activities of the bands and their fans made the island notorious. Alerted by its aura of sex and drugs, the local authority demanded expensive improvements to the hotel. It was forced to close in 1967, a group of anarchists moved in, and soon the building was home to the largest hippie commune in England. The party was shortlived: the hotel burned to the ground in 1971, cause unknown. More than 40 years on, artists lend a little glamour to Eel Pie Island, but it no longer has a dubious reputation.

Address In Twickenham, West London, TW1 3DY | **Getting there** Overground to Twickenham, then 10 minutes' walk; bus R 68 from Richmond to King Street. To see the island without setting foot on it, take a boat trip from Richmond: Apr – Sept daily | **Tip** The White Swan on the north bank of the Thames opposite the eastern tip of Eel Pie Island is a 300-year-old pub with a beer garden and good food (daily 11am – 10.30pm).

30__Fournier Street

The ghosts of Huguenots and Jewish tailors

Several rooms in the Victoria and Albert Museum are devoted to 18th-century English arts and crafts. The displays include exquisite silk fabrics, finely woven with floral patterns in delicate colours and superb Rococo embroidery. The skills to make them were brought to London by Huguenots, Protestants who were expelled from France in 1685. Many of these immigrants lived in poverty after their arrival, but hard work and talent made others wealthy. The surviving witnesses to this prosperity are solid, handsome brick houses around Fournier Street in Spitalfields. The long rows of windows in the attic storeys of such houses were installed to admit plenty of daylight for the intricate work of weaving and sewing.

After 1750, competition from Indian and French textile industries increased. Spitalfields became a poor area. The fine residences of Huguenot families were divided up into flats. In the 19th century, a new wave of immigration created a huge demand for housing: 100,000 eastern European Jews, most of them desperately poor, came to the East End, which soon became known for the quality of its Jewish tailors – and the well-lit attics were used again. When the Jewish community dispersed, immigrants from Bangladesh kept up the tradition. Shops that sold colourful saris only 15 years ago have largely given way to restaurants, but Fashion Street is home to a college of textile design, and on Sundays, young clothes designers sell their cutting-edge fashion on the Brick Lane and Spitalfields markets.

Today, the houses in Fournier Street are sought-after homes. Residents include the artists Tracy Emin and Gilbert & George. It is still worth looking out for the Huguenots' attic windows, and traces of the Jewish past remain: a closed synagogue at no. 19 Princelet Street, parallel to Fournier Street, and the lettering 'S. Schwarz' on the front of no. 33.

Address Between Brick Lane and Commercial Street, E1 6QE | Getting there Tube to Aldgate East (Circle, Hammersmith & City Line) | Tip Dennis Severs' House (18 Folgate Street, admission by reservation only, +44 (0)20/72474013, www.dennissevershouse.co.uk) is a captivating recreation of a Huguenot house as it was in the early 18th century.

31 The Fourth Plinth

No more statues of soldiers, please!

Trafalgar Square was designed as an expression of heroism and patriotism. Lord Nelson, victor over the French and Spanish fleets at the Battle of Trafalgar, stands on his column, surrounded by four proud lions. The corners of the square are marked by large plinths for monuments: an equestrian statue of King George IV in the north-east, and two generals who expanded the British Empire in India on the south side. The plinth in the north-west remained unoccupied. The intention was to honour King William IV, but he was not especially popular, and the money needed for a bronze king on a horse could not be raised.

More than 150 years after King William's death, a proposal was approved to hold a programme of temporary installations on the empty plinth. The first, Mark Wallinger's figure of Christ wearing a crown of thorns made from barbed wire, was placed at the edge of the plinth in 1999 – although life-sized, in this position it seemed small and vulnerable. Many artists who were chosen in the following years saw the Fourth Plinth as an invitation to meditate about everyday human matters in contrast to the otherwise monumental character of the square. In 2001 Rachel Whiteread made a cast of the plinth in semi-opaque resin, and placed it upside down on the stone original. Marc Quinn used Carrara marble to make a 13-tonne image of the pregnant Alison Lapper, an artist who was born without arms and with shortened legs. Antony Gormley recruited 2,400 volunteers, who each spent one hour on the plinth on 100 days in 2009. In 2012, a bronze boy on a rocking horse occupied the elevated position that was designed for an equestrian monarch.

There have been various suggestions for the future. The persons thought to deserve a permanent monument include Nelson Mandela, Margaret Thatcher and Captain Sir Tom Moore. The favourite for this honour, however, is Queen Elizabeth II.

Address Trafalgar Square, WC2N 5DN | Getting there Tube to Charing Cross (Bakerloo, Northern Line) | Tip The circular granite base of the lantern at the south-east corner of the square is hollow. It was a discreet police station with a small door, telephone and viewing slits for keeping an eye on demonstrations.

32 Fulham Market Hall
Street food under a roof

Street food, sold from outdoor stalls that spread aromas from all over the world through the London air, is a fine thing, but the local weather does not always encourage the idea. So what could be more sensible than to take the stalls off the street and put a roof over their stoves? This happened at Fulham Market Hall, which opened in 2018 in the heritage-listed concourse of what used to be Fulham Broadway underground station.

A bar in the refurbished ticket office, a coffee shop and seven small food stalls, with occasional changes of occupant, provide plentiful variety. Lovers of Asian food enjoy the rice pancakes from Sri Lanka, filled with meat, fish or vegetables, with the addition of chutney and other hot condiments to give them zing. Poke dishes from Hawaii combine a traditional meal of fish from the Pacific region with East Asian ingredients, using sustainably caught fish. For those who prefer European flavours there are kebabs and pizzas – the latter displaying more ingenuity than the standard varieties from old-fashioned pizzerias, thanks to toppings of chorizo, serrano or spicy lamb sausage, with vegan mozzarella as an option. Vegetarians and vegans are well catered for in the hall. Those with room for a dessert can try churros with sweet sauces such as melted Belgian chocolate. The operator of Fulham Market Hall succeeds in attracting stands with noticeably higher quality than the fast-food offerings at shopping centres.

The steel-and-glass roof of the ticket hall, dating from 1880, creates bright, pleasant surroundings for up to 180 diners. The brown ceramics that clad the façade on Fulham Broadway also embellish the interior. With their dark wood and green tiles, the ticket offices are especially stylish. And for days when the weather chooses to smile on London, there is a cocktail bar on the roof terrace, open at weekends.

Address 472 Fulham Road, SW6 1BY, www.markethalls.co.uk | Getting there Tube to Fulham Broadway (District Line) | Hours Mon–Thu 7am–11pm, Fri 7am–midnight, Sat 8am–midnight, Sun & bank holidays 10am–10pm | Tip For more variety than in Fulham Market Hall, take the District Line to Victoria, where the same company operates a much larger food hall with world cuisine (191 Victoria Street).

33 __ Fulham Palace

A country seat for bishops

Does the bishop of London ever look out of his window at the densely built urban environs of his house close to St Paul's Cathedral and wish he lived in the country? Until 1975, his predecessors had a palace in peaceful green surroundings near the Thames. In the year 700, they were already lords of the manor of Fulham, which then lay a few miles west of an Anglo-Saxon settlement named Lundenwic. At some stage – the first mention dates from 1141 – the manor house in Fulham became a summer residence for the bishops, who could reach their cathedral quickly by boat. Fulham Palace was a refuge from the stench and epidemics of London, and in the 20th century it became the bishops' official residence and place of work.

The palace has had an eventful architectural history. The oldest part, the Great Hall (1495), stands in a courtyard dating from the 16th century. Two beautiful early 19th-century rooms, the library and dining room, house an exhibition about the history of the manor and the museum shop. The chapel is Victorian, with some 1950s' murals and stained glass.

Ancient and rare trees beautify the park. This was originally the work of the botanist Bishop Compton (1675–1713), who collected exotic plants and was the first person in Europe to cultivate a magnolia. The gnarled holm oak, which is estimated to be 450 years old, may have been planted in the time of Bishop Grindal (1559–1570), who once presented grapes from his garden in Fulham to Queen Elizabeth. This tradition lives on in the walled garden, where the vine house has recently been restored, and a knot garden laid out in decorative shapes bounded by low box hedges in the style of Elizabethan times. On sunny days, the lawn is a popular playground and picnic spot for families. A wooden figure representing Bishop Compton looks down benignly on the fun from the 'Bishop's Tree' sculpture.

Address Bishop's Avenue, Fulham, SW6 6EE, www.fulhampalace.org | Getting there Tube to Putney Bridge (District Line), then a few minutes' walk west on the bank of the Thames | Hours Museum Mon–Thu 12.30–4.30pm, Sun noon–5pm, in winter Mon–Thu 12.30–3.30pm, Sun noon–4pm, botanical garden daily during daylight hours, walled garden daily 10.15am–4.15pm | Tip The Drawing Room Café (daily Apr–Oct 9.30am–5pm, Nov–Mar 9.30am–4pm) in the palace serves breakfast, lunch and afternoon tea in elegant rooms with comfortable armchairs or on the garden terrace.

34 The Gas Lamp in Carting Lane

Sewers and street lighting

More than 200 years after gas lighting was first introduced on London's streets, in Pall Mall in 1807, 2,000 gas lamps still provide flickering illumination in areas such as Mayfair and Covent Garden. The strangest of them has burned day and night for 100 years in a ravine-like street called Carting Lane next to the Savoy Hotel. In 1894, Joseph Edmund Webb patented his 'sewer gas destructor lamp'. Its purpose was to burn methane. It is sometimes said that the lamp in Carting Lane uses the vapours generated in the toilets of the luxury hotel next to it, and that the street should therefore be renamed 'Farting Lane'. It is true that a sewer, to which the Savoy is connected, runs down the lane to the Embankment, but since the 1950s the lantern has operated on normal gas.

Webb's invention was not intended to replace the gas produced from coal in a gasworks, but to have an additional safety benefit. During its operation with conventional gas, it drew explosive methane, which was a hazard to the public, out of the sewers and burned it along with the gas from the mains supply. The problem and Webb's solution were consequences of the construction of sewers in London by the engineer Joseph Bazalgette. Following the 'Great Stink' in summer 1858, when the stench from the Thames made it impossible for Parliament to sit, over 400 miles of sewers were built. The system drained into the river east of London. The project included the building of the Embankment road. Two of the original pumping stations still exist: Abbey Mills to the north and Crossness to the south of the Thames, the latter a superb industrial monument with impressive cast-iron architecture. The engine there is under steam on several days a year (www.crossness.org.uk). Bazalgette's work put an end to the cholera epidemics that killed thousands of Londoners in the mid-19th century.

Address Carting Lane (WC2R 0DW) connects the Embankment and The Strand | Getting there Tube to Embankment (Bakerloo, Circle, District, Northern Line) | Tip On Victoria Embankment at the end of Northumberland Avenue is a memorial to Joseph Bazalgette.

35 Gasholder Park
Mirrors of change

To walk around the circle of black iron columns, surrounded by bright reflections of grass, trees and buildings from highly polished mirrors, is slightly disorienting. Gasholder Park may be small, but visually it is a big experience.

Gasholder no. 8 was built in the 1850s and stayed in service until 2000. Then its 16 hollow cast columns and two horizontal strips of iron lattice-work were restored, placed near the bank of the Regent's Canal and used as the framework for a new park. Within the ring of columns you tread the paving of a covered circular walkway whose supports are clad in mirror glass. The underside of the walkway roof, too, is a mirror, reflecting a kaleidoscope of impressions as you pass beneath it. Blue sky or clouds, your own moving shape, the green bank and lawn in the centre, the young shrubs that bound the circle – it's a parade of light and colour, like riding a carousel.

The contrast between matt ironwork and the dazzling mirrors stands for the transformation of the old King's Cross railway yards into a hip quarter.

Next to gasholder no. 8 stand the 'Siamese triplets' numbers 10, 11, and 12, three interlocking iron skeletons that now encircle luxurious flats. The prices for the wedge-shaped homes within started at £800,000 for a studio flat and rose to several million for a penthouse. The developers were obliged to build more than 600 affordable homes nearby, but the gasholder flats are pie-slices of prime property, with a spa and private cinema for residents.

Gasholder number 8, however, is for everybody. Paths and landscaped gardens link it to the canal bank, with a view of moored narrowboats. Across the canal lies a patch of much wilder greenery, the Camley Street Natural Park, and fans of historic ironwork can walk along King's Boulevard to admire more of it in the German Gymnasium, a sports hall of 1865, now a restaurant.

Address On the Regent's Canal near Stable Street | Getting there Tube to King's Cross-St Pancras (Circle, Northern, Piccadilly, Victoria Line) | Hours Always accessible | Tip Across Stable Street, in the Granary Building of 1851, now home to Central Saint Martins Art and Design College, is the trendy and justly popular Bombay-style eatery Dishoom. It's worth the wait for a table: the House Black Daal tastes sensational (+44 (0)20/74209321, www.dishoom.com).

36_ God's Own Junkyard

Rolling Scones and an assault on the eyeballs

Walthamstow lies far out in the north-east of Greater London, but the trip takes only 20 minutes from the West End by Tube, and is rewarded by an astonishing spectacle, an explosion of colour. The home of God's Own Junkyard is a modest factory hall on an industrial estate. Inside the hall, every corner is crammed full of bright neon signs. Winking and flashing advertisements for restaurants, nightclubs, bars and motels adorn every wall, and are reflected in disco mirror-balls. They promise all kinds of services, from sushi to 'beer, girls and porn'. This is not a museum, but a showroom for collectors, and thousands more examples of neon art await purchasers in storerooms. A 20-strong team of restorers puts the sparkle back into old neon signs and also makes new ones – a craft that few people master in the age of LED lighting, as it requires a great deal of skill to bend the glass tubes.

Dick Bracey founded the company in the 1950s. His son, Chris, became a true artist in neon, producing eye-catching and creative signs in the 1960s. Many were commissioned for the sex and strip-tease clubs of Soho in its seedy days, and a few were made for Hollywood films, including *Blade Runner*, and Stanley Kubrick's *Eyes Wide Shut*. Chris Bracey's works became collectors' items, finding purchasers said to include Lady Gaga and Elton John.

The fitting acoustic background to these garish wares is rock music. It entertains customers at the tables of the Rolling Scones Café, which have been squeezed in between the neon exhibits. In these surroundings, a desire for something stronger than afternoon tea is understandable, so cocktails are served, and in neighbouring units on the estate no fewer than three craft beer breweries and a gin distillery have set up shop. All are open at weekends, approximately at the same times as the Junkyard, turning this gritty corner of Walthamstow into an extremely trendy scene.

Address Unit 12, Ravenswood Industrial Estate, Shernhall Street, E17 9HQ,
www.godsownjunkyard.co.uk | Getting there Tube to Walthamstow Central (Victoria Line),
turn right at the exit, cross Hoe Street, straight ahead along St Mary Road and Church
Path, right into Orford Road, left into Summit Road, and to the metal gate at the end; it's
about a 12-minute walk | Hours Fri & Sat 11am–9pm, Sun 11am–6pm | Tip The walk to
the Junkyard passes the old village centre of Walthamstow with its church, a 15th-century
half-timbered house, and the Vestry House Museum, where the first British-made petrol-
driven car, from 1894, is displayed.

37 __ The Golden Boy

Gluttony, fire and body-snatching

The Great Fire of 1666 destroyed more than 13,000 houses, 87 churches and St Paul's Cathedral. A large part of the historic City of London was burned to the ground, and as many as 70,000 lost their homes. One of the points where the spread of the flames was finally contained on the fourth day was the junction of Cock Lane and Giltspur Street – a spot known as Pye Corner. Today, this place is marked by a gilded wooden figure of a chubby little boy.

Who was to blame for the disaster? 'Foreigners!' said some, and an innocent Frenchman was lynched. The godly had a different explanation: the Great Fire, they claimed, was punishment for the sin of gluttony, as the inscription at the feet of the Golden Boy states. The fact that the fire broke out in a bakery in Pudding Lane and came to a halt at Pye Corner, of all places, was seen as an obvious confirmation of this pious theory.

The sins associated with this spot continue with a further affront to traditional Christian morals: a second, longer inscription tells us that the Golden Boy was originally placed on the façade of a tavern called The Fortune of War. This drinking hole was a haunt of the infamous body snatchers, also known as 'resurrection men', who stole corpses and sold them for dissection. In the back room of the tavern they displayed the bodies they had dug up in order to sell them to surgeons from the nearby St Bartholomew's Hospital. The usual source of corpses was the execution of criminals, but in the late 18th century felons were more often transported to Australia than hanged. As a result, bodies for teaching and medical research were in short supply, and the resurrection men's business flourished until 1832, when doctors gained the right to dissect donated bodies – usually of paupers from workhouses. Further along Giltspur Street towards Newgate, a stone watch house dated 1791 stands next to St Sepulchre's churchyard. Here, guards kept watch to prevent the grisly trade in corpses.

Hosier Lane

Address Corner of Giltspur Street/Cock Lane, SE23 3PQ | Getting there Tube to
St Paul's (Central Line), at the exit left to Cheapside, then along Newgate Street to
Giltspur Street on the right | Tip The Viaduct Tavern at the corner of Giltspur Street
and Newgate caters to the sins of gluttony and drunkenness with hearty meals and the
excellent ales of Fuller's brewery.

38 — The Greenwich Foot Tunnel

Under the Thames and off to Scotland

Visitors who have seen the outstanding sights in Greenwich – the National Maritime Museum, the Royal Observatory on the 0° meridian, the Queen's House and the Cutty Sark – have not exhausted all the attractions there. In a circular brick building with a glass dome close to the Cutty Sark, you can descend to a tunnel, cross under the Thames and look back over the water from Island Gardens on the north bank to the splendid architecture of Greenwich and its park.

Tunnels have been built beneath the river in many places in London. The first of them, the work of Marc Brunel and Isambard Kingdom Brunel from 1825 to 1843, connected Limehouse on the north bank with Rotherhithe on the south bank. This was also the world's first tunnel beneath a river, and more were built under the Thames in the 19th century. They served Tube trains and obviated the need for technically challenging bridges across a wide river on which tall ships sailed.

The Greenwich Foot Tunnel opened in 1902 to allow dockers to reach the warehouses and port basins on the Isle of Dogs, a peninsula on the north bank formed by a loop of the Thames. The tunnel is 15 metres below the surface and 370 metres long. It was made from cast-iron rings covered by a layer of concrete and 200,000 white tiles. Broad winding stairs lead down to it below the circular buildings at either end. Since 1904, lifts have operated. They were renewed recently, again for the benefit of those who work on the north bank – nowadays employees of financial institutions around Canary Wharf. Many go to work by bike, ignoring the instructions to dismount in the tunnel. If they don't feel like going to the office when they emerge on the north side, they can simply carry on pedalling: the tunnel is part of national cycle route no. 1, which goes all the way from the south coast at Dover to the Scottish Highlands.

Address Greenwich Foot Tunnel, SE10 9NN | Getting there DLR to Island Gardens (north bank) or Cutty Sark (south bank) | Hours 24 hours daily | Tip In The Old Brewery next to the Royal Naval College, excellent craft beers are on tap.

39_ The Grenadier

Cosy, until the ghost appears

There are some astonishing corners of London where the feeling of being in a throbbing capital city suddenly vanishes. One such place is in Belgravia, close to the roaring traffic of Knightsbridge. Leave the imposing stone façades of Wilton Crescent for the smaller Wilton Row, then turn left – and all at once a village scene confronts you. A 300-year-old pub beneath trees is painted in patriotic red, white and blue. The inn sign depicts a soldier in a bearskin cap, and a bright red sentry box stands to the left of the steps that lead up to the front door.

The Grenadier Guards, founded in 1656 as a bodyguard for King Charles II, were stationed in a barracks on this site until 1818. In that year, the officers' mess was converted into a pub, and little has changed since. The bar in the wood-panelled room at the front has its original pewter top. In the Wellington Room behind, hearty pub meals are served. Photos, prints and newspaper cuttings on the walls celebrate military tradition and the pub itself: Grenadier Guards pose for a snapshot in front of Buckingham Palace, and an old print shows a Waterloo Dinner, the annual celebration of Napoleon's defeat that was given by the Duke of Wellington for his comrades nearby in his London residence.

It is likely that the Duke himself drank here with his officers. Their carousals were not always marked by good behaviour. During one drinking bout, a subaltern is said to have been caught cheating at cards. His comrades beat him so savagely that he died on the cobblestones in front of the pub. More details are not known, but the incident is thought to have happened in September. In this month an icy chill is reported to haunt the building. Footsteps and groans can be heard, and a mysterious figure moves silently through the rooms. The banknotes that guests have signed and pinned to the ceiling of the front bar are meant to propitiate the ghost.

Address 18 Wilton Row, SW1X 7NR, +44 (0)20/7235 3074, www.grenadierbelgravia.com | **Getting there** Tube to Hyde Park Corner (Piccadilly Line) | **Hours** Daily noon–9.30pm, Sun until 9pm | **Tip** Apsley House (Hyde Park Corner, Apr–Oct Wed–Sun 11am–5pm, Nov–Mar Sat & Sun 10am–4pm) has a fine interior, an exquisite art collection and memorabilia from the first Duke of Wellington's military career.

40__The Hardy Tree
Human jam

Given its location next to the high-speed tracks to Paris, the cemetery park around Old St Pancras Church is unexpectedly atmospheric. Pancras is said to have been martyred in Rome in 303. Tradition claims that a church dedicated to him stood here in late Roman times, which would make Old St Pancras London's oldest Christian place of worship.

The strangest sight in the cemetery is a 150-year-old ash: the Hardy Tree. Tombstones have been placed around its trunk like the spokes of a wheel. It commemorates people whose bones were disturbed and jumbled in the 1860s to make way for the railway. The architect's apprentice tasked with moving the graves was the later novelist Thomas Hardy, whose poem 'The Levelled Churchyard' includes these lines: *We late-lamented, resting here, are mixed to human jam, and each to each exclaims in fear, I know not which I am!*

The poem continues in a satirical vein, imagining that the inscription from the headstone of a teetotaller now stands over the bones of a drunkard, and that the bones of a virtuous virgin might be mixed up with those of a prostitute when bodies are resurrected on the Day of Judgement.

The deceased who were desecrated in this way may find some consolation in the neo-Gothic monument that was erected for them when the cemetery was made into a park in 1877, and by the company of some famous people. Here lie the remains of the composer Johann Christian Bach, youngest son of the great Johann Sebastian, and of Mary Wollstonecraft, an early advocate of women's rights. Wollstonecraft's daughter Mary Shelley, who wrote the original *Frankenstein* novel, met her husband, the poet Shelley, in this cemetery, and they planned their elopement at her mother's grave. The striking funeral monument designed by Sir John Soane for himself and his wife is said to have inspired the design of the K2 telephone box (see ch. 51).

Address Pancras Road, NW1 1UL | Getting there Tube to Mornington Crescent (Northern Line), or King's Cross-St Pancras (several lines) | Hours Daily until dusk | Tip Although Old St Pancras Church is heavily marked by Victorian restoration, signs of its early history remain: Roman tiles in the walls, possibly from a military camp, and a stone in the chancel that might date from the 7th century.

41_Hawksmoor's Pyramid

An enigma in the churchyard

St Anne's Church in Limehouse is one of 50 that were to be con-
structed for the growing population of London according to an act of
Parliament in 1711. Only twelve were built, six of them by Nicholas
Hawksmoor (1661–1736), who had worked under the aegis of Sir
Christopher Wren on St Paul's Cathedral, Chelsea Hospital and
Hampton Court Palace.

Hawksmoor evolved his own idiosyncratic interpretation of the
Baroque style, revealing his interest in Gothic and classical architecture and his liking for dramatic effects of light and dark, mass and
space. The striking tower of St Anne's Church has outsized corner
buttresses and a top storey turned by 45 degrees. The clock, the highest on a London church, used to chime the quarter hours for ships in
the surrounding docks, as the tower was within sight of the official
time signal in Greenwich. Small pyramids surmount the east end of
St Anne's.

In the large churchyard stand tall plane trees, benches, scattered
gravestones and a three-metre-high stone pyramid, partly covered in
moss and lichen. The south side bears the inscription The Wisdom
of Solomon and a weathered coat of arms on which it is just possible
to make out a unicorn. In the absence of hard evidence on the origin
of the pyramid, speculation has run riot. Its dimensions do not fit
the most popular theory, that it was destined for the church tower.
Two prominent contemporary authors associated with London, Peter
Ackroyd and Iain Sinclair, have woven stories around a possible connection to the occult. Are Hawksmoor's six churches located in the
form of a pentagram? Is there a mystic background to the architect's
known fascination with geometry? Does the pyramid in some way
express the beliefs of Freemasons? Or is it simply a left-over architectural component that fitted nowhere and has remained to adorn
and add atmosphere to the churchyard? Nobody knows.

Address Newell Street, E14 7HP | Getting there DLR to Limehouse | Hours Churchyard open in daylight hours | Tip The actor Sir Ian McKellen owns a historic pub that serves food on the banks of the Thames in Limehouse: The Grapes (76 Narrow Street, +44 (0)20/79874396).

42 The Head of Invention
Inspiration for designers

Though human genius with its various inventions with various instruments may answer the same end, it will never find an invention more beautiful or more simple or direct than nature, because in her inventions nothing is lacking and nothing superfluous. This quote by Leonardo Da Vinci is cast in bronze on a sculpture entitled *The Head of Invention* in front of the Design Museum in Kensington.

Eduardo Paolozzi created this three-metre-high head in 1989 and placed it on wooden planks. Originally the work stood close to the river in the street Shad Thames. From there, the Design Museum moved to its new premises in 2016 – and of course the bronze head had to move too, as its concept and the quote perfectly match the topic of design and the daring engineering of the museum architecture. The building was constructed in 1962 to house the Commonwealth Institute, and is described in its listing by Historic England as one of the most important examples of Modernism in London. It is especially notable for its spectacular roof in the shape of a hyperbolic parabola.

On the rear of the *Head of Invention*, the sculptor included some machine parts – possibly representing the mechanism of thought. Paolozzi is reported to have taken inspiration from the head of a famous compatriot, the Scotsman James Watt (1736 – 1819), inventor of the first efficient steam engine. Compatriot? – yes, the artist's name is deceptive. Paolozzi (1924 – 2005), the son of an Italian immigrant, was born in a suburb of Edinburgh and is regarded as a pioneer of Pop Art. He worked in many different media and created several public works of art that can still be seen in London. The best-known are his colourful mosaics on the walls of Tottenham Court Road underground station and a bronze sculpture of Isaac Newton, based on William Blake's depiction, that stands in front of the British Library on Euston Road.

Address 224–238 Kensington High Street, W8 6AG | **Getting there** Tube to High Street Kensington (District/Circle Line), then walk five minutes west along the High Street | **Tip** A visit to the Design Museum is always worthwhile for excellent exhibitions (daily 10am–6pm, www.designmuseum.org).

43 Highgate Wood

The remains of an ancient forest

Extensive woodland once covered the high ground in the north of London, and large areas of the adjacent counties of Hertfordshire and Essex. The 28-hectare Highgate Wood is a relic of these forests, and of great ecological value. This is because it is not the result of planting, but a patch of ancient woodland with great biodiversity.

In Roman times the wood was a source of fuel for pottery production: parts of a kiln that was in operation in the first century were excavated in Highgate Wood. In the Middle Ages this land, like the whole of Highgate, was owned by the bishops of London, who set up a toll barrier – a 'high gate' – on the main road heading north from the capital. In later centuries the woods were leased to foresters who coppiced the trees, mainly hornbeam, harvesting them every 10 to 30 years, either for fuel or poles used in making fences. Highgate Wood was then an area of commercially exploited underwood in the shade of tall oak trees. In 1886, it passed into the ownership of the City of London, which opened it to the public for recreation.

Today, it is a nature reserve. Thirty species of birds, including kestrels, nest in the wood. Seven kinds of bat and more than 400 species of moths and butterflies are also at home here. The most common trees are oak, hornbeam and holly. Fallen trunks and boughs are left on the ground so that fungi can grow, and the rotting wood nourish beetles and other insects. The facilities also include a children's playground, a sports field and the Pavilion Café, but the most valuable resource for local residents are the walks beneath mature trees, the woodland air, and the peaceful surroundings. An inscription on a drinking fountain at the crossing of paths quotes lines by the poet Samuel Taylor Coleridge:

Drink, pilgrim, here. Here rest! And if thy heart be innocent, here, too, shalt thou refresh thy spirit.

Address Between Archway Road and Muswell Hill Road, N10 3JN | **Getting there** Tube to Highgate (Northern Line); at the crossroads with traffic lights by the tube station turn into Muswell Hill Road; the woods are 100 metres ahead on the left | **Hours** Daily 7.30am–dusk, Pavilion Café daily from 9am | **Tip** A 10-minute walk from the tube station via Southwood Lane is the attractive village centre of Highgate, where you'll find a historic pub, The Flask (77 Highgate West Hill, www.theflaskhighgate.com).

44 Holland Park

More than a Dutch garden

In the north-west of Holland Park, two huge bronze tortoises crawl beneath the style of a sundial. The work of the sculptor Wendy Taylor, they could be a metaphor for the way that changes sometimes happen very slowly.

Until 1952, this 23-hectare park in the middle of the city was the private property of an aristocratic family. Some 400 years ago, Sir Walter Cope, chancellor of the exchequer under King James I, built himself a mansion here in wooded grounds more than two miles west of the City of London. The house later passed into the possession of the earls of Holland and was named Holland House. The estate included pasture land as well as the woods and gardens around the mansion. For 100 years from the mid-18th century, Holland House was a meeting place for high society and politicians, where the great parliamentarian Charles James Fox spent much of his childhood. The illustrious visitors included Sir Walter Scott, Lord Byron and Charles Dickens. Then the building fell into disrepair, suffered severe bomb damage in the Second World War, and was sold by the owners to the Royal Borough of Kensington and Chelsea.

Over decades, the ruins of Holland House and its grounds became one of London's finest parks. The east wing of the house was saved and made into a youth hostel. The Dutch Garden that survived from the days of glamour was restored, and now presents a blaze of colour in summer. The Japanese-style Kyoto Garden with its flowering cherry trees, magnolias and cedars was added. In the wooded northern section of the park, daffodils and rhododendrons flower in spring. There is a café and covered arcades for rainy days. Tennis courts, children's playgrounds, open-air chess and opera performances beneath a canopy provide entertainment. Thus an aristocratic estate became a place of recreation for one and all, and backpackers sleep in the remains of the mansion.

Address Abbotsbury Road, W8 6LU | **Getting there** Tube to Holland Park (Central Line) | **Hours** Daily 7.30am until 30 minutes before dusk | **Tip** In 1866, the artist Lord Leighton built himself a dwelling and studio with an opulent Moorish-style interior (Leighton House, 12 Holland Park Road, see www.rbkc.gov.uk for opening times after restoration). The gardens and houses of an artists' colony in the neighbouring streets are also a fine sight.

45 The Horniman Museum

Varied fun for all ages

When the tea merchant Frederick Horniman made his house in south London into a museum in 1890, he declared his intention of 'bringing the world to Forest Hill', as he had collected wonders and curiosities from every continent. Eleven years later a new building was constructed to hold the growing number of exhibits, and further extensions were needed. The Horniman Museum now possesses 350,000 items, and presents them in a family-friendly way that surely meets the founder's intentions.

Perhaps the most famous department is the room with stuffed animals, especially the 'overstuffed walrus', which was prepared 100 years ago by an over-enthusiastic taxidermist who seemingly did not know that the animal should have jowls and loose folds of skin. The World Gallery displays 3,000 ethnographic exhibits, comparing different cultures by looking at specific themes. The items range from a Tuareg camel saddle to English amulets that protect the wearer against witches, displayed beneath a canopy of kites and banners from Guatemala, China, Afghanistan and elsewhere. The rooms devoted to the arts include a magnificent 19th-century 'apostle clock' from the Black Forest, on which the figures of the 12 apostles parade past Jesus every afternoon at four o'clock.

There's also plenty to do and see in the six-hectare hilltop park. The historic bandstand commands a wonderful view of the skyline of inner London, the zoo has goats, alpacas, sheep and hens, the aquarium specialises in breeding jellyfish, and there's also a tropical butterfly house. The gardens have a variety of biotopes in which exotic and native plants grow, and 12 sundials are spread along an educational trail. Refreshments to round off the visit are taken in the café or, in good weather, on the outdoor terrace. This is next to a beautiful conservatory of cast iron and glass, which originally stood in the garden of the Horniman family home in Croydon.

Address 100 London Road, Forest Hill, SE23 3PQ, www.horniman.ac.uk | Getting there
Train to Forest Hill, 10–15 minutes from London Bridge or Victoria, then a 5-minute walk
(signposted) | Hours Museum: daily 10am–5.30pm; park: 7.15am–dusk; Animal Walk
daily 12.30–4pm; free admission to museum, aquarium £4.50, butterfly house £6 | Tip
At the bottom of the hill on London Road, a bike path on the right follows the route of a
disused railway, and the Horniman Nature Trail passes beneath trees for half a mile.

46___Horse at Water

A restful sight at Marble Arch

The north-east corner of Hyde Park is a spot that has seen its share of uproar. On Sundays, any eccentric or hothead with firm opinions and a loud voice can harangue the public at Speaker's Corner. Countless criminals were hanged on Tyburn gallows. Now the name of the place derives from a triumphal arch of Carrara marble. It was designed by John Nash as an entrance to Buckingham Palace, but had to be moved when the palace was extended in 1851 – the famous balcony for royal waving marks the approximate site. In contrast to public executions and the Sunday shouting, a bronze sculpture of a horse's head now imparts a soothing mood to Marble Arch.

The sculptor Nic Fiddian-Green has loved the form of a horse's head since he was young. His first inspiration was a work in the British Museum, the horse of the moon goddess Selene from the sculptures on the pediment of the Parthenon. Today Fiddian-Green's outsized horses' heads have been installed in many different countries. Horse at Water, placed between a 1960s' fountain and Nash's arch in 2010, is 10 metres high and weighs 17 tons. In what appears to be a miraculous balancing act, it rises above a flat metal base that represents the surface of the water from which the horse is drinking.

Traffic thunders all around, as Marble Arch is one big roundabout for buses, but the horse's head is a perfect motif to make a transition from the surrounding bustle to Hyde Park. Horses have a close historic connection with the park: Hyde Park Barracks is the base of the Household Cavalry regiment, which rides daily to the changing of the guard on Horse Guards' Parade and has ceremonial functions at royal occasions. The park was once the place for fine ladies to show themselves in their carriages, and the broad track called Rotten Row that forms the southern boundary of the park is still used by riders.

Address North-east corner of Hyde Park, W1H 7AL | **Getting there** Tube to Marble Arch (Central Line) | **Tip** The Serpentine Gallery and Serpentine Sackler Gallery in Kensington Gardens (Tue–Sun 10am–6pm) put on changing exhibitions of contemporary art. Each year a renowned architect is invited to design a temporary Serpentine Pavilion.

47 Inner Temple Garden
For lawyers and everyone else

700 years ago the area called The Temple, between Westminster and the City of London, belonged to the Templar Knights. After the dissolution of this military religious order in 1312, the land came into the possession of the guilds and schools of lawyers that are now known as the Inns of Court. Two of the four existing inns, the Middle Temple and Inner Temple, still have a walled enclave for their halls, libraries and legal chambers. Historic buildings are grouped around courtyards and gardens, as in a monastery or the colleges of Oxford and Cambridge.

On weekday afternoons the Inner Temple allows visitors to pass through its splendid wrought-iron gate, dating from 1730, into the garden. The flower beds to the left and right of the gate are densely planted from spring until autumn – from the first tulips in March, followed by poppies and foxgloves that bloom in tastefully co-ordinated shades of red and purple in summer, to late-flowering dahlias. Beyond the gate is a raised terrace flanked by rose beds. Roses have a special significance in the Inner Temple and were cultivated here as long ago as the 14th century. In Shakespeare's *Henry VI* this garden was the setting for the start of the Wars of the Roses, when representatives of the rival houses of York and Lancaster picked white and red roses respectively as their symbols. The planting of the long beds in front of the brick building on the left makes reference to this.

Stone steps with Mediterranean plants on either side lead down to the lawn. Ahead, tall plane trees screen the garden from the roaring traffic of the Embankment. Before the construction of the Embankment in the 1860s, the garden extended right down to the banks of the Thames. This area is now a shady spot where snowdrops herald the arrival of spring. A round pond with a little fountain and some benches makes a pleasant place to sit.

Address Inner Temple, 1 Mitre Court, EC4Y 7BS, access from The Strand/Fleet Street, e.g. via Middle Temple Lane, www.innertemple.org.uk | **Getting there** Tube to Temple (District, Circle Line) | **Hours** Mon–Fri 12.30–5pm; for other opening times see website | **Tip** A few yards west of Middle Temple Lane, at 218 The Strand, the company Twinings has sold fine teas for 300 years.

48 Isabella Plantation

An enchanted garden in the wide green park

In the great expanse of Richmond Park, once a royal hunting ground, it goes without saying that green is the dominant colour, as areas of grass alternate with woodland. In contrast to this, a delightful wooded garden on the south side of the park, Isabella Plantation, displays bright hues almost throughout the year. Camellias bloom here early in the year, while in April and May colour is provided by rhododendrons, a notable collection of azaleas, and bluebells, which form a dense, fragrant carpet beneath the trees. In summer, a huge variety of garden flowers line the paths, ponds and watercourses, and in autumn the leaves of native and exotic trees glow red and yellow.

Isabella Plantation was created from 1830 onwards with the planting of oaks, beeches and sweet chestnuts on a 17-hectare site that was marshy in places. In the 1920s, 50 rare species of azaleas were brought from Japan, but it was only in the 1950s that the garden became the sensuous display that visitors see today. Two streams and three ponds were dug out, and the diversity of the shrubs and trees was increased.

Today, ecological gardening is the watchword. The banks of the streams, mature woods – about 250 trees remain from the period before 1830 – and ponds are a biotope for bats, 50 kinds of beetle, 130 different moths and butterflies, and 70 bird species. The banks of ponds were made less steep to enable amphibians to move in and out more easily. Dragonflies hover over the water, and birds take refuge in the reeds. For most visitors the conspicuous beauty lies not in the fauna but in flowering plants, skilfully laid-out paths, and magical spots such as the circular Still Pond. What about the name Isabella? Commemoration of a gardener's lovely daughter, perhaps? Probably not: the obsolete word 'isabel' once denoted the faded yellow of vegetation on infertile ground. What a transformation!

Address Richmond Park, TW10 5HS | **Getting there** Parkbus from mid-Apr to late Oct, see www.royalparks.org.uk for timetable; train from Waterloo to Putney, bus 85 from Putney High Street to Warren Road, then a 15-minute walk (signposted) | **Hours** Daily round the clock, with restrictions in Feb and Nov (see website for current information on visiting) | **Tip** Richmond Park is perfect for taking a long walk in what feels like open countryside.

49__James Smith & Sons

Where a gentleman buys his umbrella

Is there a lovelier shop front anywhere in London? Above windows framed in dark wood, the name James Smith & Sons – Established 1830 is announced with a flourish. The initials are radiant in red and gold, and the strip of brass beneath with beaten lettering still has a shine. The signage advertises products that sound like props from a Victorian murder mystery: life preservers, dagger canes, sword-sticks above one window, riding crops, whips, Irish blackthorns next to it. Sticks are still sold here, but umbrellas are the mainstay of the business.

James Smith founded his shop in Foubert Place, Soho, and man-ufactured umbrellas in a workshop at the back. In 1857, he moved to the present address in New Oxford Street, where there is still a repair shop in the cellar. In those days, every gentleman carried a stick, whether a white cane or something more rustic for days in the country. Umbrellas became increasingly common in Europe from the 17th century, but the first man to carry one in England regularly did so surprisingly late, from about 1750. He was pelted with mud by coachmen and sedan-chair bearers, who thought the invention a threat to their business.

At James Smith, still a family-run company, the interior lives up to the façade. Above the counter, a gallery with a glass balustrade serves as the accounts department. The wooden shop fittings of draw-ers and cupboards are 150 years old. They display a fine product range: umbrellas with the head of Sherlock Holmes or a duck on the handle, conservative models all in black, floral patterns and lace for ladies, folding umbrellas in gaudy colours. The sticks come with a huge variety of knobs, and even integrated corkscrews or whisky flasks. Every wish can be fulfilled, but the management does issue one warning: 'It is inadvisable to lend your James Smith umbrella to even your closest friend.'

Address 53 New Oxford Street, WC1A 1BL | Getting there Tube to Tottenham Court Road (Central, Northern Line) | Hours Tue–Sat 10.30am–4.30pm | Tip Though under threat from redevelopment, Denmark Street is still a centre of the music business, with shops selling instruments.

50__Jamme Masjid Mosque
A house of three religions

The building at the north-west corner of Brick Lane and Fournier Street has a remarkable history. Today it stands in 'Banglatown' – the marketing name for the rows of curry houses at the southern end of Brick Lane. This district, Spitalfields, belongs to Tower Hamlets borough, where almost 40 per cent of the population are of Bangladeshi origin. During the 1970s, as their numbers increased in the East End, they founded several mosques, one of them in an existing place of worship.

Spitalfields was an immigrant quarter 300 years ago. Huguenots, that is Protestants who had been expelled from France, settled here and built a church on Brick Lane in 1743. In time the Huguenot community was assimilated and lost its distinct identity. In 1809 the church was made over to a society for converting Jews to Christianity. This mission was unsuccessful, and after only 10 years the building became a Methodist chapel. In the late 19th century, tens of thousands of Jews from eastern Europe moved into the area and converted the old church into the Machzeike Hadass Synagogue in 1898. In the following decades Spitalfields was a poor but lively Jewish quarter. After the Second World War the Jewish community gradually moved away, and the synagogue building was shut up. It reopened in 1976 as the Jamme Masjid Mosque.

A tall, shining cylinder of steel that glows in changing colours at night, a substitute for a minaret, is the outward sign that a third religion has now taken possession. Inside the building, the old church pews were removed, the upper galleries in the prayer hall enlarged, and basins for ritual ablutions installed. A survival from the first church is a sundial on the Fournier Street side, inscribed *umbra summus*: 'we are shadows'. This reference to the insubstantiality of human life raises the question: is the mosque the final chapter in this story?

Address Brick Lane, E1 6QL | Getting there Tube to Aldgate East (Circle, Hammersmith & City Line) | Tip The few traces of Jewish culture in this area include a 24-hour bagel shop (Beigel Bake, 159 Brick Lane) and a synagogue in Sandy's Row, an alley south of Spitalfields Market.

BRICK LANE JAMME MA

51 The K2 Telephone Kiosk
The prototype of a famous design

Behind the wrought-iron gates of the Royal Academy of Arts stands the very first example of the red telephone box called K2. This one-off item was made of wood for a competition in 1924, as the earlier model, K1, had been rejected.

The designer of K2 was Giles Gilbert Scott (1880–1960), a scion of a well-known dynasty of architects. At the age of 22, he was awarded the commission to build the Anglican Cathedral in Liverpool, and has a strong presence on the Thames with his two unmistakable power stations at Bankside (now the Tate Modern) and Battersea. For the miniature architecture of the phone box, Scott turned to the formal repertoire of classical building. His careful design gave it a shallow dome and fluted window frames. For the colour, he proposed silver, but the General Post Office opted for red and installed 1,700 steel-built K2 phone kiosks, one of which stands opposite the prototype. The 200 surviving K2s are all protected monuments.

With its height of 2.74 metres and a weight of 1250 kilos, K2 was too expensive, but alternatives made of concrete (K3), with a built-in stamp vending machine (K4) and of plywood (K5) failed to catch on. In 1935, Scott produced a simplified version: K6, 30 centimetres shorter and 500 kilos lighter than K2, with a teak door; 60,000 of them were manufactured. K6 is plainer and has eight rows of windows on each side, with the middle window in each row wider (K2 has six rows of three windows, all the same size). K6 became a design classic, so popular that its successor, K8, did not appear until 1968. Around 11,000 K6 boxes still stand in Britain, and a considerable number can be seen abroad; 2,260 of them are listed heritage structures. They are not all identical. Look out for the crown in the pediment: since 1953 it has been a depiction of St Edward's Crown, the one used for coronations, rather than a stylised 'Tudor' crown.

Address Burlington House, Piccadilly, W1J 0BD | **Getting there** Tube to Piccadilly Circus (Bakerloo, Piccadilly Line) | **Tip** The Royal Academy of Arts founded in 1768 has its own art collection and puts on outstanding changing exhibitions. Its cafés are good places to take a break.

52 The Kindertransport Monument

The place where 10,000 Jewish children arrived

The group of bronze figures in front of the south entrance to Liverpool Street Station depicts five children of various ages. The youngest, a girl, sits on a suitcase with a teddy bear in her hand. The boy to her right holds a satchel and a violin case. The older girl behind him is not keeping an eye on the smaller ones at this moment, as they are all looking in different directions. They are waiting to be collected, and the group is about to split up. The names of cities on a length of railway track behind them show the children's places of origins: on one side Cologne – Hanover – Nuremberg – Stuttgart – Düsseldorf – Frankfurt – Bremen – Munich, on the other Danzig – Breslau – Prague – Hamburg – Mannheim – Leipzig – Berlin – Vienna.

Between December 1938 and September 1939, almost 10,000 Jewish children arrived at Liverpool Street via the Netherlands and the port of Harwich. Following the attacks on synagogues and German Jews instigated by the Nazi government on the 'Kristallnacht' ('night of broken glass'), 9 to 10 November 1938, the British government allowed Jewish children up to the age of 17 to immigrate, provided that a foster family and a benefactor willing to give a bond of £50 were found. The first to come were 196 children from an orphanage that had been burned down in Berlin. The German authorities allowed the children to take one suitcase and one bag, containing no valuables and only one photo. No adult escort and no farewells at the railway station were permitted. The 10,000 children were dispersed around Britain, and few ever saw their parents again. Frank Weisler, who was born in Danzig (now Gdansk) in 1929 and came to his grandmother in London with a Kindertransport, later studied architecture in Manchester and became a sculptor in Israel. He made the monument in London and similar works in Hoek van Holland, Gdansk and Berlin.

Address Hope Square, EC2M 7QN, in front of Liverpool Street Station | Getting there Tube to Liverpool Street (Central, Circle, District, Hammersmith & City, Metropolitan Line) | Tip More information can be found on the website www.kindertransport.org. W. G. Sebald, a German writer who spent most of his life in England, made it the subject of his strange and brilliant novel *Austerlitz*.

53　Limehouse Basin
Post-industrial London

Canals played an important part in the early stages of the Industrial Revolution. The construction of Limehouse Cut began in 1766, enabling traffic from the River Lea, which flows into the Thames from the north, to reach the quays in the City of London more directly. The Regent's Canal, a long arc around the north side of central London, opened in 1816, transporting goods that had come along the Grand Union Canal from the Midlands to the harbour basin in Limehouse. This linked the entire network of English canals and navigable rivers to the London docks on the Thames, and thus to the world's biggest port and its global trade.

Today, boats can still pass along Limehouse Cut and the Regent's Canal to the old dock that is now called Limehouse Basin, but freight transport on these routes came to an end in 1969. The quays and warehouses fell into decay until the redevelopment of the whole huge area of London's Docklands began. New housing was built from 1993 onwards, and a declining area with a bad reputation gradually became fashionable. Limehouse Basin now provides moorings for expensive motorboats, ocean-going yachts, a few historic sailing barges and a number of narrowboats – the gaily painted traditional vessels of the canals.

Expensive flats, cafés and shops now occupy sites where coal from the north-east of England or wood from Finland and Norway was once unloaded. In the north-eastern corner of the basin stands a relic of the days of goods transport: the brick accumulator tower, built in 1869 to power hydraulic cranes, swing bridges and lock gates. The celebrity chef Gordon Ramsey has his restaurant The Narrow next to the lock gate, offering diners a view of the Thames from the terrace – a scene of modern urban life, though not entirely without natural features, as cormorants, herons and even kingfishers join Ramsey's customers here to enjoy some fish.

Address Narrow Street, E14 8DP | Getting there Overground and DLR to Limehouse | Tip 250 metres east of the lock is a riverside pub dating back 450 years: The Grapes, which is part-owned by the actor Sir Ian McKellen (76 Narrow Street, www.thegrapes.co.uk).

54 Lincoln's Inn

A tranquil refuge for lawyers

To pass through the gateway on Chancery Lane is to leave the noise of London behind and to step into an older, quieter world. Mature plane trees spread their boughs over beautifully kept lawns. A varied ensemble of historic buildings borders courtyards where the atmosphere is reminiscent of an ancient university – and indeed Lincoln's Inn, one of four institutions of the legal profession that possess their own enclave in central London, was once a place where law students lived. Those who wish to qualify as a barrister must be members of these 'inns of court', which are a kind of professional association whose responsibilities include training young lawyers. Like the nearby Gray's Inn, Inner Temple and Middle Temple, Lincoln's Inn is home to barristers' chambers and collegiate institutions such as a chapel, hall and library.

Lincoln's Inn is first mentioned in documents in 1422, but probably existed decades earlier. The gatehouse dates from 1520, the Old Hall, which is used for meals, debates and festivities, from the year 1490. The scholar and Lord Chancellor of England Thomas More, who enrolled in 1496, is one of many eminent persons who dined in this hall. Five prime ministers – Pitt the Younger, Gladstone, Asquith, Thatcher and Blair – were members of Lincoln's Inn.

Visitors can walk in the courtyards but not enter the buildings with the exception of the Gothic chapel, completed in 1623 and restored 60 years later by Wren, also a member of the Inn. It became an early casualty of air warfare in 1915, when bombs dropped from a zeppelin destroyed two stained-glass windows. The Stone Buildings in classical style running north along Chancery Lane date mainly from the 18th century, the red-brick segment of the library and Great Hall from the 19th century. These parts combine to form a harmonious ensemble, and a refreshing contrast to the neighbouring streets.

Address Chancery Lane, WC2A 3TL | Getting there Tube to Chancery Lane (Central Line) | Hours Courtyards Mon–Fri 7am–7pm, chapel Mon–Fri 9am–5pm | Tip Dealers in the bazaar-like subterranean Silver Vaults sell an extraordinary range of silver products, some of them extremely precious (53–64 Chancery Lane, Mon–Fri 9am–5.30pm, Sat 9am–1pm).

55 Little Ben
Off-message since Brexit

The year 2017 saw the start of a thorough restoration for Big Ben – officially called the Elizabeth Tower, as strictly speaking the nickname applies only to the great bell, not the whole tower. The world-famous landmark was shrouded in scaffolding and sheets, and to the regret of Brexiteers was not able to chime at midnight (Central European Time) on 31 January, 2020, when the United Kingdom left the European Union. Big Ben's lesser-known little brother was not, however, a suitable spot to celebrate Brexit, as it is overtly pro-European.

Little Ben has a modest height of nine metres. It was made from cast iron in 1892 by Gillett & Johnston, a family company that still produces and repairs clocks for churches, town halls and rail stations. The site, on a noisy traffic island, is unappealing, but proximity to Victoria Station is an essential part of the concept. The miniature tower was a rendezvous for French travellers returning home on trains to the Channel ports, which used to depart from Victoria. The French oil company Elf Aquitaine made a donation for restoring Little Ben in 1981 'as a gesture of Franco-British friendship'. Two lines of verse on the tower entitled *Apology for Summer Time* attest to good relations between the two countries at that time:

'My hands you may retard or may advance,
My heart beats true for England as for France.'

This refers to the time difference between Britain and Continental Europe, and the debate about putting UK clocks forward and back by one hour in spring and autumn, respectively. A plan that this clock would show BST all year round, and thus in winter the correct time in Paris but not in London, was never implemented. Little Ben patriotically keeps to British time in all seasons. The EU has decided in principle to abolish the change to summer time, but rules made in Brussels no longer apply at Victoria Station.

Address Next to Victoria Station at the junction of Vauxhall Bridge Road and Victoria Street, SW1E 5EA | **Getting there** Tube to Victoria (District, Circle, Victoria Line) | **Tip** Two minutes' walk away on Victoria Street, visitors have a superb view from the (clock-free) tower of Westminster Cathedral (Mon–Fri 9.30am–5pm, Sat & Sun 9.30am–6pm).

56 The Lloyd's Building

Futuristic, yet a monument

It is rare for a building less than 35 years old to be listed by English Heritage as one of half a million protected monuments. And for a work by a living architect to be included among the 10,000 structures that are officially designated as grade one, i.e. 'of exceptional interest', is not merely unusual, but unique. Richard Rogers achieved this distinction with his Lloyd's Building of 1986, which gained grade-one listing in 2011.

Seen from Leadenhall Street, the Lloyd's Building towers above its neighbours and rebukes their conservative, early 20th-century stone façades with expanses of grey metal. External glass lifts, water pipes and ventilation ducts rise up the shiny surface, and conspicuous blue cranes for the window cleaners perch on the roof. The design principle is that of the Centre Pompidou in Paris, which made Rogers and his former partner Renzo Piano famous: everything that is hidden in conventional architecture – lifts, staircases, the building services – is boldly displayed on the outside, in order to create an uncluttered, adaptable interior space.

When it was inaugurated, the 88-metre-high building (95 metres with the cranes) was all the more provocative for being the new home of a revered 300-year-old institution. Lloyd's of London evolved from Lloyd's Coffee House, which by 1688 had become a place for merchants and sea captains to exchange news and, increasingly, to conclude insurance agreements. Lloyd's is not a company but an association of independent insurers. Trading is done on the ground floor of a 60-metre-high atrium, around which three office towers and three towers for building utilities are grouped. The interior is by no means entirely high-tech in appearance: the Committee Room on the 11th floor, originally a dining room designed by the great 18th-century architect Robert Adam, was transferred here from the old Lloyd's Building.

Address 1 Lime Street, EC3M 7HA, www.lloyds.com | Getting there Tube to Monument (Circle, District Line) | Hours Open only during the Open House Weekend in Sept | Tip Opposite the Lloyd's Building stands a new high-profile work by Rogers, the 224-metre Leadenhall Building (2014), known as the 'Cheesegrater' thanks to its sloping façades.

57 London Stone

The city's mythical foundation stone

One of London's strangest monuments lay neglected for decades behind bars and dirty glass in the façade of a down-at-heel 1960s' office block. When redevelopment of the site began in 2016, the stone was displayed in the Museum of London, then returned to its rightful historic place.

London Stone is a fragment of limestone measuring approximately 50cm by 40cm by 30cm – all that remains of a larger stone associated in legend with the beginnings of the city. According to one story, it is a relic of a stone circle built by the giants Gog and Magog on the site now occupied by St Paul's Cathedral. A 12th-century chronicle tells that Brutus came to London from the ruins of Troy, and was instructed by the goddess Diana to build a temple, of which London Stone was the altar. The mystic poet William Blake believed that druids performed human sacrifices upon it. Others claimed that King Arthur drew the sword Excalibur from this stone, while modern New Agers take it to be the mid-point of a ley line connecting St Paul's with the Tower of London. A more sober interpretation sees the block as the central Roman milestone from which distances were measured.

The facts are scanty. The first written reference dates from the 11th century. In the Middle Ages great significance was ascribed to the stone: debts were paid and oaths taken there. It was the landmark at which, in Shakespeare's telling, the rebel Jack Cade proclaimed himself ruler of London in 1450. Until the road was widened in 1742, London Stone stood on the south side of the street, was then placed in the wall of St Swithin's Church, and survived the destruction of the church in 1941. The site of St Swithin's is now 111 Cannon Street. When the old office block was torn down in 2016, the stone was examined. No new insights into its origins resulted, but it is now presented in a setting that befits its status.

Address 111 Cannon Street, EC4N 5BP | Getting there Tube to Cannon Street (Circle, District Line) | Tip Beneath the new Bloomberg Building (12 Walbrook, near London Stone) the remains of a Roman Temple of Mithras are presented in an excellent multimedia show (Tue–Sat 10am–4pm, Sun noon–5pm, www.londonmithraeum.com).

58 Lord's Cricket Ground

A sacred site for fans of the summer sport

Wembley for football, Wimbledon for tennis, Lord's for cricket. Lord's is older than the other two, as the first recorded match here took place on 22 June, 1814. Two hundred years ago, aristocrats liked to play cricket and wagered enormous sums of money on the outcome. From 1787, the businessman Thomas Lord made ground available for this purpose on the site that is now Dorset Square. Later he moved to a place south-east of the present stadium, but had to make way for the new Regent's Canal. The third Lord's, 'the home of cricket', is for the most part a nondescript modern structure – with two notable exceptions. The Media Centre, a great viewing pod that was built in boatyards using marine technology, won the Stirling Prize for Architecture in 1999. The splendid Pavilion at the opposite end dates from 1890. Here, club members watch matches from the tiered balconies, or through the windows of the venerable Long Room beneath portraits of great cricketers of the past. Many members proudly wear the red-and-yellow ('bacon and egg') striped blazer of the ground's owner, the Marylebone Cricket Club. When rain stops play, they can see the treasures in the world's oldest sports museum, including a stuffed sparrow that was hit by a ball in 1936, and the small urn containing the 'ashes of English cricket', a trophy made in 1882 following a catastrophic defeat at the hands of the Australian team.

Although the number 111 has a special aura – Tolkien's Lord of the Rings opens with Bilbo Baggins' eleventy-first birthday party, for example – in cricket it is unlucky, and is called a 'Nelson' because Admiral Nelson is said to have had one arm, one eye and one leg (in fact he had two legs). When the score of a team or batsman is 111, or 222 or 333, the superstitious expect disaster. To avert misfortune, the umpire David Shepherd used to stand on one leg if this score was reached.

Address St John's Wood Road, NW8 8QN | Getting there Tube to St John's Wood (Jubilee Line) | Tip A pleasant stroll along the Regent's Canal, which can be reached 400 metres south or east of Lord's, leads west to the canal basin at Little Venice or east to Regent's Park.

59 M. Manze

Eel, pie and mash in Peckham

London is heaven for food fashionistas. It seems that every culinary trend in the world comes to the city. But there's bad news too: a decline in the number of outlets that cook the city's own traditional dishes. These are old-fashioned eel, pie and mash shops, which numbered about 100 in the mid-20th century. Now there are only around 30 of these establishments, and they are not found in central London. Their staples are jellied eel, and minced beef pie served with mashed potato and 'liquor' – a parsley sauce.

In 1902, Michele Manze, whose parents came to England from the south of Italy in 1878, opened a shop at 87 Tower Bridge Road. This establishment, London's oldest eel and pie shop, is still in business. Manze established his fifth and last shop in Peckham in 1927. The other three have closed down. In Walthamstow, another family now runs an outlet under the name Manze. It was established by Michele's brother Luigi, and is a heritage-listed building thanks to its original interior fittings, which date from 1929.

Since the retirement of Michele's grandchildren in 2019, Manze's two shops have been run by the fourth generation. All dishes are freshly prepared each day. The eels are boiled in water with vinegar and herbs. When the liquid cools, the natural proteins in the eel congeal to form the jelly. For the pies, pastry is kneaded by hand and filled with beef that has been minced on site. The mashed potato does not come ready-made from a packet, and the liquor is made to the family recipe, which is a well-guarded secret.

The shop burned during riots in Peckham in 1985. When it reopened in 1990, the family recreated the interior in the traditional style with wooden benches and tiles. The original façade, with its gold lettering and green tiles, has been preserved, and for just £5 or £6 customers can still get a nutritious meal in the accustomed quality.

Address 105 High Street, Peckham, SE15 5RS, +44 (0)207 277 6181, www.manze.co.uk | Getting there Train to Peckham Rye (16 minutes from London Bridge), turn left into Rye Lane, then right into the High Street | Hours Mon 11am–2pm, Tue–Thu 10.30am–2pm, Fri 10am–2.15pm, Sat 10am–2.45pm | Tip Like a spaceship that has landed in the suburbs, Peckham Library stands 50 metres from Manze's. In 2000, the architect Will Alsop won the coveted Stirling Prize for this work – it's worth taking a look inside too.

60__ The Marx Memorial Library
Lenin, trade unions and the Spanish Civil War

A short walk from the City, but ideologically as distant as it could possibly be, a remarkable institution occupies a handsome 18th-century building on Clerkenwell Green: the Marx Memorial Library and Workers' School, founded in 1933. The left-wing history of the premises is older than this. From 1872 the radical London Patriotic Club was based there. In 1892, the Twentieth Century Press started to print socialist literature in the building, and here Lenin corrected the proofs of Iskra ('Spark'), the newspaper of the Russian Social Democratic Party, while living in London in 1902–1903.

Today the building is crammed from the cellars to the roof with 48,000 books, archives of activists and trade unions, piled-up pamphlets and posters, and memorabilia of the workers' movement displayed almost like holy relics. In the meeting room is a tattered banner of the British battalion that fought in the Spanish Civil War. Now behind glass, it was once laid on the coffins of the fallen. The courtyard is a shrine to these fighters, with a small statue of a bare chested worker holding a rifle. The library staff sit in front of a mural entitled The Worker of the Future Clearing away the Chaos of Capitalism: a heroic figure reduces great buildings to rubble, watched by Marx, Engels, Lenin and the British Socialists Robert Owen and William Morris. A visit to the building by Marx himself is not recorded, but his daughter Eleanor certainly frequented it.

A partitioned-off corner is presented as the office in which Lenin worked. On show here is a coat given to Harry Pollitt, leader of the British Communist Party, by his Bulgarian counterpart when he attended a winter congress in Moscow without warm clothing. Yet the library is more than an array of devotional items. It is a place for serious research and a riposte to the shiny towers of the banks.

Address 37A Clerkenwell Green, EC1R 0DU, www.marx-memorial-library.org.uk |
Getting there Bus 55 or 243 from Tottenham Court Road to Clerkenwell Road / St John
Street | **Hours** Wed–Thu 11am–4pm by appointment. See website for seminars and
lectures. | **Tip** After the dusty air of the library, a pint in the Crown Tavern, 47 Clerkenwell
Green, goes down well. The story that Lenin first met Stalin here in 1905 is unconfirmed.

61___ The Molehill

How a victorious king was laid low

High on his horse, King William III dominates the park in St James's Square. The sculptor depicted him as a young military commander. This is William of Orange, who married the daughter of King James II and seized the throne from his father-in-law in 1689, at the invitation of the English aristocracy. He defended the Netherlands against the mightiest ruler of the day, Louis XIV of France, led Protestant armies in European wars, and is celebrated in Northern Ireland by Loyalists as 'King Billy', the victor over Irish Roman Catholic forces.

A mole brought him down. On 21 February, 1702 he went out for a gallop on his new mare in the park at Hampton Court. The horse stumbled over a molehill, William was thrown from the saddle, and died from his injuries 15 days later. The equestrian statue shows him riding at a stately pace, not a gallop – but what is that little heap beneath the horse's rear left hoof? Is it a support, placed there to stabilise the monument, or could it be a molehill?

Whatever the sculptor intended, St James's Square is a majestic place, laid out in the 1660s by the Earl of St Albans, with permission from Charles II to build residences worthy of high-ranking aristocrats. In the 1720s it was home to seven dukes and seven earls. The plaques on the buildings name three prime ministers who lived at number 10. Several fine 18th-century interiors remain, for example at number 4, now the Naval and Military Club (Lawrence of Arabia and Rudyard Kipling were members). Since 1841, number 14 has been the seat of the London Library, a private institution with a long list of illustrious subscribers, including Charles Darwin and Sir Arthur Conan Doyle. But St James's Square is not only for high society: the garden is open to everyone, and in good weather, workers from nearby offices and building sites eat their lunch under the gaze of King William.

Address St James's Square, SW1Y 4LG | **Getting there** Tube to Piccadilly Circus (Bakerloo, Piccadilly Line) | **Hours** Garden: Mon–Fri 10am–4.30pm | **Tip** 5th View, a café and cocktail bar on the fifth floor of the enormous Waterstone's book shop, offers good quality at reasonable prices, with a view across the West End rooftops (203 Piccadilly, Mon–Sat 9am–10pm, Sun noon–5pm).

62 Mudchute City Farm
Animals for urban children

When children from the East End were evacuated to the country during the Second World War, shocking ignorance came to light. Some of them were amazed at the size of cows, which they had imagined to be no bigger than dogs. Today they are better informed, as London is blessed with a number of educational farmyards, of which Mudchute City Farm on the Isle of Dogs is the largest at 13 hectares. The curious name 'Mudchute' goes back to the 19th century, when docks were built in the north of the Isle of Dogs. The soil and Thames mud excavated during this work were deposited on the southern part of the peninsula, creating an unplanned but extremely fertile biotope. The port area has now become part of the shiny new Docklands with its towers for financial institutions and expensive apartments at Canary Wharf and Canada Water. The district to the south of it, formerly housing for dockers and their families, was redeveloped, and the mud heaps were converted to a park and farmyard in the 1970s.

As you walk southwards from the Crossharbour stop on the Docklands Light Railway, the scene changes completely within a few minutes. The postmodern high-rise architecture recedes into the background, meadows appear, hedgerows line the path, and you have soon reached Mudchute City Farm, where admission is free. It has pens for donkeys, sheep and llamas and a pond for geese and ducks. Turkeys wander about with impressive dangling wattles, golden pheasants strut in their cages, and horses graze in a paddock. For smaller children, there are rabbits, guinea pigs and a playground, for the older ones a riding school, and a café caters to the parents. Greedy goats are hand fed on carrots, and various events familiarise the young generation with life on a farm – valuable entertainment and education, as the Isle of Dogs is a district where poor families live.

Address Pier Street, E14 3HP, www.mudchute.org | Getting there DLR to Crossharbour; from the station walk across the supermarket car park | Hours Park always open, for farm see website | Tip From the next DLR station, Island Gardens, it is a short walk to the river bank for a fantastic view of historic Greenwich.

63__ The Naked Ladies

Unexpected frolics by the Thames

Walkers heading east from Twickenham on the banks of the River Thames are greeted after about two minutes by an unexpectedly erotic sight: at the top of a mound of mossy rocks stands a naked goddess, in a chariot pulled by rearing, wild-looking horses with flared nostrils. Meanwhile, an enigmatic drama is being played out at her feet: nymphs look up with gestures of supplication; one of them seems about to cast herself despairingly into the pool beneath, while another is being hauled on to the rocks.

Who are these beauties? The goddess may be Venus, her companions sea nymphs. They are generally known as the Naked Ladies, and their story is as remarkable as their presence in a municipal park. A swindling financier named Whitaker Wright commissioned the figures for the park of his grand house in Surrey, and an Italian sculptor made them from fine Carrara marble. By the time the ladies arrived in England, Wright's fraudulent dealings had been exposed, and in 1904 he swallowed a cyanide capsule in the Royal Courts of Justice immediately after being found guilty.

When Wright's assets were sold, a wealthy Indian, Sir Ratan Tata, bought the marble figures to adorn the grounds of his stately residence, York House in Twickenham. He employed landscape gardeners to build a fountain to display them, and in the years before the First World War they were the backdrop to garden parties attended by royalty and high society. In 1918, the estate passed to the local council, which still has offices in Tata's mansion. The Naked Ladies were thought unseemly in a public park, but found no bidders at auction. During the Second World War they were covered in grey slurry, due to fears that the white marble shining in the moonlight would attract German bombers. Today, cleaned and restored, the ladies disport themselves in the arrangement conceived by the landscape gardeners in 1909.

Address Riverside, TW1 3DD | Getting there Train from Waterloo to Twickenham | Tip 400 metres east along the river, the Orleans House Gallery holds changing art exhibitions in the Baroque Octagon Room – all that remains of the mansion that once stood there; attached is the Stables Café (Tue – Sun 10am – 5pm, www.orleanshousegallery.org).

64 Neal's Yard

Alternative lifestyle and Monty Python

Between 1974, when the fruit, vegetable and flower markets moved out, and the 1980s, when Covent Garden began to attract fashionable shops and crowds of tourists – at a time, that is, when the area was still pleasantly shabby and rents were low, unconventional people breathed new life into a triangular back yard. The warehouses in Neal's Yard had served the flower market and were still home to a company that made theatrical weapons and armour.

In 1978, an organic bakery with a café opened in Neal's Yard. It was joined by a cheese shop and Neal's Yard Remedies, which sold natural cosmetics and health products. Soon the courtyard had become the little island of alternative lifestyle that it still is today. The brick warehouse walls have been painted in gaudy colours – purple, orange, bright yellow. Seats have been placed around old metal barrels planted with bamboo and shrubs. Health and beauty treatments with a mystic touch are available in the Holistic Room, the hairdresser specialises in dreadlocks, and courses about how to gather wild food in woodlands and pastures can be booked.

Neal's Yard Remedies, now a retail chain, is still present, and the Neal's Yard Dairy, sourcing artisan cheesemakers, has moved around the corner into Short's Gardens. In its early days, the shop struggled to gain a good reputation. John Cleese came in one day to find empty shelves. Production problems meant that yoghurt was on sale, but no cheese at all. The creative result of this mishap was Monty Python's celebrated cheese-shop sketch. A plaque in the yard records that Monty Python lived here. The recent opening of a chic wine bar in Neal's Yard suggests that the spreading commercialisation of Covent Garden may one day overpower the green, alternative ethos of this enclave, but the Wild Food Café is still selling its burgers filled with root vegetable jerk and smoothies enriched with Irish moss.

NEAL'S

Address Between Short's Gardens and Monmouth Street, WC2H 9AT | Getting there Tube to Covent Garden (Piccadilly Line) | Tip Those who prefer traditional British fare to vegetarian wholefood will find excellent fish and chips at the Rock and Sole Plaice (47 Endell Street, Mon–Sat noon–8pm). The Monty Python sketch is on YouTube.

65___ The Niche from Old London Bridge

Stones that were admitted to hospital

One of the few remaining fragments of London Bridge is a semi-circular covered niche with a bench. It stands in the courtyard of Guy's Hospital and has a permanent occupant – the poet John Keats, who studied medicine here and, cast in bronze, now pores over his books between the flower beds.

This weather-beaten little structure is not part of the medieval fabric of the bridge, but dates from restoration work in 1760. Until that date, shops and houses crowded the length of the bridge and limited the width of the road. These additions were then removed, and 14 niches were added to provide shelter for pedestrians. When Old London Bridge was finally demolished in 1831, Guy's Hospital acquired one of the sturdy stone shelters and placed it next to an outer wall as a place for psychiatric patients to sit. It became known as the 'lunatick chair'. Two more niches survive in Victoria Park in Hackney. The first London Bridge was built in Roman times close to the present bridge and possibly repaired during the Anglo-Saxon period. The Normans constructed a wooden bridge, and in 1176 Henry II commanded a new one to be built in stone. At its centre was a chapel dedicated to St Thomas Becket, who had been martyred on Henry's orders. A drawbridge could be raised to let tall ships pass through, and fortified gates guarded the north and south approaches. As a warning to enemies, traitors' heads were placed on spikes above the gates. The broad piers of the 19 bridge arches restricted the flow of river water so much that dangerous rapids were created, and the pent-up Thames upstream often froze over.

It is well worth taking a look around the grounds of the hospital that Thomas Guy founded in 1721. However, to see the immediate successor to Old London Bridge, you have to go to Lake Havasu City in Arizona, where it was re-erected in 1971.

Address St Thomas Street, SE1 9RT | Getting there Tube to London Bridge (Jubilee, Northern Line) | Tip In the attic of St Thomas's Church opposite Guy's Hospital, the Old Operating Theatre has been preserved in its original 19th-century condition, along with an apothecary's shop, the Herb Garret (9a St Thomas Street, daily 10.30am–5pm).

66 Nunhead Cemetery
Romantic decay

The graves in Nunhead Cemetery evoke contradictory feelings: beholders may be moved by the romantic decay, or outraged that such finely carved stone memorials could be so neglected. At the inauguration in 1840, an orderly 20-hectare cemetery was planned on a 60-metre hill with a view of the city centre. At that time, Nunhead was a rural community that supplied vegetables to the population of London. The cemetery was one of the 'magnificent seven' necropolises, run on a commercial basis by limited companies. Expanses of lawn, paths flanked by oak and chestnut trees, and a neo-Gothic chapel promised eternal rest in worthy surroundings – and satisfactory dividends for shareholders. By the 1960s, however, the operator saw no further prospect of making profits and stopped all maintenance work. A well-kept place of memorial turned into wilderness, the lawns into woodland with impenetrable thickets beneath tall trees.

Today, Nunhead is a nature reserve and a place of recreation for joggers and dog walkers rather than a site of pious remembrance. Climbing plants obscure magnificent stone tombs. The tree trunks and roots have toppled slabs and crosses. Graceful angels have fallen from their plinths. Beautifully carved urns lie scattered on the ground under ivy and brambles.

The Friends of Nunhead Cemetery carry out urgent rescue work, and a few splendid monuments remain: near the imposing main entrance, an obelisk commemorates the Scottish Martyrs, who demanded political reform around the year 1800, and were transported to Australia. From here, an avenue leads to the chapel. Keep right and follow the southward curve of the path to reach some superb graves, such as that of the Figgins family, in neo-classical style with a canopy on columns. A right turn here leads to West Hill, where a gap in the trees reveals a distant view of St Paul's Cathedral.

Address Linden Grove, SE15 3LP, www.fonc.org.uk | Getting there Train to Nunhead from Victoria Station (15 minutes), then a 5-minute walk via Oakdale Road and Linden Grove to the main entrance | Hours Daily 8.30am–4.30pm (4pm in winter); see website for info on guided tours | Tip The Ivy House at 40 Stuart Road is a community pub; from the south-east cemetery gate turn right into Limesford Road, straight ahead to Borland Road, then right into Stuart Road (www.ivyhousenunhead.com).

67__One New Change

A free vista of London and St Paul's Cathedral

A passage cut into the façade of One New Change directly faces St Paul's Cathedral. On entering, you walk to the lift and are whisked upwards – and enjoy a spectacular view of the cathedral dome, reflected in glass walls to left and right as the lift ascends. The sight is breathtaking, but up on the observation deck you'll catch your breath again as your gaze sweeps over the rooftops of London – southwards across the river to the Millennium Wheel, the glass prism of The Shard, but above all to the sublime cathedral dome opposite.

For admission to the viewing platforms of St Paul's Cathedral and The Shard, visitors pay a steep price; One New Change, by contrast, charges nothing. This may be a wise concession, as the bulky building, opened in 2010, is controversial. It could hardly have a more sensitive site: St Paul's Cathedral is of course one of London's most prominent landmarks, and its dome, which barely survived the hail of German bombs, represented a symbol of national resistance during the Second World War.

Directly opposite this revered holy place, One New Change is a shopping centre topped by 31,000 square metres of office space. The opaque frontage of brown-tinted glass slanting at various oblique angles resulted in the nickname 'stealth bomber'. Prince Charles, who has often engaged in architectural polemics, tried to prevent this design, even though the architect, Jean Nouvel, was honoured by Prince Charles' own family in 2001, when Nouvel was awarded the Royal Gold Medal. To be fair, Nouvel's building has more modest dimensions – 8 storeys and a height of 34 metres – than its predecessor on the site. Like it or not, One New Change unquestionably gives visitors a wonderful free view. And those who want to spend some money can do so in the rooftop restaurant and cocktail bar, or in any of the 60 shops and eateries beneath.

Address 1 New Change, EC4M 9AF, www.onenewchange.com | Getting there Tube to St Paul's (Central Line) | Hours Daily 6am–midnight | Tip Also on the roof terrace are works of art salvaged from the previous building, including a mosaic by the Russian artist Boris Anrep, representing Ariel from Shakespeare's *The Tempest*.

68__Orbit

An observation tower on the Olympic site

The 2012 Olympic Games were planned on the principle that the biggest party ever held in London should not be followed by a hangover. Instead of leaving decaying, unused stadiums, which were the legacy of mega-events in Athens, Beijing and South Africa, the intention was to transform industrial wasteland into a large park on the banks of the River Lea, business and entertainment districts and pleasant residential areas. The sports venues were partly dismantled, leaving a downsized aquatics centre, the velodrome and the main stadium, which became the new home of West Ham United FC in the 2016–2017 football season. Up to 6,800 homes in five new districts are to be built by 2030 – and in the middle of all this will stand an eye-catching visitor attraction, a sculpture 115 metres high that doubles as a viewing tower.

The tower, produced through a collaboration of the engineer Cecil Balmond and the artist Anish Kapoor, is officially called Arcelor-Mittal Orbit. The billionaire Lakshmi Mittal made a large contribution, including steel that his company produced with 60 per cent recycled content in accordance with the Olympic project's declared aim of sustainability. The structure looks like a white-knuckle looping ride, made of red tubular steel wrapped around a central support. Two viewing platforms at the top present a 30-kilometre panorama across the whole of London for up to 5,000 visitors daily. They can descend via 455 steps circling around the main pillar with a view of the sculptural forms, or take a 40-second, adrenalin-kick orbit on a 178-metre-long slide – or sedately use the lift.

Critics have variously damned this 'snake that swallowed a broomstick' and 'vainglorious sub-industrial steel gigantism', or praised its organic shape as 'a network of bulging red arteries' and 'a generous drunken party animal'. The popularity of Orbit as a viewpoint suggests that the party has successfully been held without a hangover.

Address South Plaza, Queen Elizabeth Olympic Park, E20, www.arcelormittalorbit.com | Getting there DLR or Tube to Stratford (Central, Jubilee Line) | Hours Mon–Fri 10am–5pm, Sat & Sun 10am–6pm | Tip Boat trips in the Queen Elizabeth Park on the River Lea run from Easter to October, daily noon–5pm on the hour.

69 The OXO Tower
Architecture as advertising

When you leave the lift on the eighth floor and find yourself in the reception area of a posh restaurant, the magic words are 'viewing terrace': if you make it clear that you have not come for an expensive meal, the staff will point the way to a small space high above the south bank of the Thames, where everyone may enjoy a wonderful view free of charge. Boats pass below, and straight ahead the London skyline is spread out for landmark-spotting: Charing Cross Station and Waterloo Bridge on the left, the British Telecom tower in the background, Somerset House directly opposite, to the right Blackfriars Bridge and St Paul's Cathedral, all mirrored in the sloping glass wall behind you. Most of the terrace is reserved for restaurant tables, but at certain times of day you can simply drink a cup of coffee here without breaking the bank.

The whole building has gastronomic origins. The brand name OXO for beef stock-cubes was invented in 1900 by Liebig's Extract of Meat Company, which was an official sponsor of the 1908 Olympic Games in London and gave the product to all competitors. During the First World War, OXO cubes were part of the emergency rations for all British soldiers. In 1928, the company built a cold store and production facilities on the Thames, to which meat was delivered directly from South America. The Art Deco building had a slender tower, but planning permission to attach neon advertising for OXO was refused. The architect's solution was a vertical arrangement of three windows on each side of the tower: the top one O-shaped, the middle one an X, at the bottom another O, and they are all lit up at night.

The OXO tower was renovated in the 1990s. The two lower storeys now accommodate design shops and galleries. Above these are apartments; at the top is the high-class restaurant. Just don't ask the chef whether he uses OXO cubes.

Address Barge House Street, SE1 9GY, www.oxotower.co.uk | Getting there Tube to Southwark (Jubilee Line) | Hours Tower Restaurant Tue–Sun noon–10pm | Tip For reasonably priced meals and galleries selling art and craftwork, go to Gabriel's Wharf immediately west of the OXO Tower.

70 Paddington Street Gardens

Keep the city clean and green

Marylebone is close to Regent's Park, but itself has few green spaces as a refuge from the traffic. One of these is the charming park to the south of Paddington Street, with a small extension on the north side, that was laid out as a cemetery for St Marylebone parish church in 1733. Burials here ended in 1857, by which time there were 80,000 graves on the site. Since 1885 it has been a park, but is still consecrated ground, and some signs remain of its former use. Almost all tombstones were taken away, but one mausoleum has such fine stonework that it was left in place. A fading inscription records that Richard Fitzpatrick erected it for his wife Susanna, who died in 1759 aged 30.

The well-kept park has a glorious collection of tall London plane trees, which shield it from an adjacent high-rise residential block. Shrubs and flower beds – cherry blossom and laburnum in spring, wonderful rose beds in summer – provide a display of colour for many months of the year. There is also a children's playground. In summer, parents can rent a deckchair while their offspring romp, or get some exercise themselves playing open-air table-tennis. A sculpture shows that some children in past centuries were not as lucky as modern kids – or is it a sentimental advertisement for child labour? The small statue by the Italian artist Donato Barcaglia, presented to the parish of Marylebone in 1943, is entitled The Street Orderly Boy, i.e. a street cleaner. He sits cutely on a pedestal, polishing his shoe.

Near the entrance to the park is a cycle-hire station, but Paddington Street is marred by fumes from heavy traffic. In an attempt to improve this, a Marylebone Low Emission Neighbourhood has been declared. One of its projects aims to plant greenery linking the two parts of the garden, choosing species of trees that effectively improve the air quality.

148

Address Paddington Street, W1U 5QA | Getting there Tube to Baker Street (Bakerloo, Circle, Jubilee Line) | Hours Daily 7am–dusk | Tip Leave the gardens by the Moxon Street entrance in the south-east to see how prosperous Marylebone appeals to foodies: here are Ginger Pig, selling high-class bacon and charcuterie, Fromagerie with its fine groceries and café, the chocolate shop Rococo and the upmarket café Aubaine.

71 The Peabody Estate in Whitecross Street

150 years of social housing projects

'Peabody Trust' can be seen on residential estates in many parts of London. It is a charity, founded in 1862 by George Peabody in response to a critical shortage of housing. At this time, journeys by public transport from the suburbs to places of work near the city centre such as the docks were too expensive for most workers. Overcrowding and disease in inner-city slums were the consequence.

Peabody had already made a fortune in America as a wholesaler when he came to London in 1827 and multiplied his wealth in the banking business. He later invested shrewdly in American railways and was an active philanthropist on both sides of the Atlantic who endowed his trust in London with half a million pounds, a truly enormous sum at that time. The Peabody Trust built accommodation with high ceilings and large windows to provide light and air, as well as wash-houses and water closets for hygiene, and let them for reasonable rents. The first estate was built in 1863 in Spitalfields. Within 25 years, the Peabody Trust constructed 5,000 homes, including those in Whitecross Street in 1883. The architecture, though solidly handsome, is austere in a way that matches the past and present regulations for tenants – cycling and skateboarding, ball games and music are prohibited in the courtyards, which have just a smattering of greenery. Sober, clean and orderly have been the watchwords for 150 years.

Until the 1970s, two flats shared a wash-house and WC in Whitecross Street. Though small by modern standards, the rooms compare favourably with most council housing of the 1960s and 1970s. Today, the Peabody Trust administers 20,000 apartments in London. A statue behind the Royal Exchange has commemorated its founder since his death in 1869.

Address Whitecross Street, EC1Y 8JL | Getting there Tube to Barbican (Circle, Hammersmith & City, Metropolitan Line) | Tip Delicious street food adds an international touch to the otherwise basic market (Mon–Fri 10am–5pm, www.bitecross.co.uk) in Whitecross Street.

72 Peckham Levels

A car park, garish and creative

What do you do with a huge multi-storey car park when it becomes surplus to requirements? Imaginative repurposing or demolition? The former option was chosen in Peckham, a district notable – even by the standards of London – for its ethnic diversity: around half of the area's residents have African or Caribbean heritage. Immigrants from Eastern Europe, China, Vietnam and South Asia are also well represented, alongside their white British counterparts.

In recent years, some parts of Peckham have become hip and affluent. The first sign that things were happening in the area was the opening in 2000 of the library, a post-modern structure that earned its architect, Will Alsop, the Stirling Prize – the most prestigious British award in this field. In 2009, Frank's Cafe opened on the roof of the redundant car park, attracting a young crowd during the summer months. Trendy cocktails at sunset with a stunning view of Alsop's library and the skyline of the City of London were irresistible attractions.

The car-parking storeys beneath the cafe were transformed into the Peckham Levels, a project to promote local creative enterprises. Levels 1 to 4 are home to 100 small businesses, start-ups of all stripes, ranging from jewellery and fashion designers to makers of musical instruments and a dance studio. The dimensions of the former parking spaces determine the layout of the co-working offices and studios that now occupy them.

Garishly painted stairwells lead up to the public levels 5 and 6, where mirrored glass and murals create a highly colourful environment for bars, street-food stalls offering everything from vegan Caribbean to regional Chinese dishes, hairdressers and beauty salons, a yoga workshop and a children's playground. At weekends and late into the evening, dance classes, exhibitions, markets and live music breathe life into the old concrete construction.

Address 95A Rye Lane, SE15 4ST, www.peckhamlevels.org | Getting there Train to Peckham Rye (16 minutes from London Bridge), left into Rye Lane and across the road; the entrance is to the right of the Peckhamplex cinema | Hours Mon–Wed 10am–11pm, Thu–Sat 10–1am, Sun 10am–midnight | Tip Meals from Senegal and the Caribbean, food from South America and Africa, and clothes from all over the world are sold at Rye Lane Market (Mon–Sat 10am–6pm).

73__The Piccadilly Line

Design and architecture in the Tube

The Piccadilly Line is dark blue on the famous map of the London Underground, that much-admired work of art that makes a complex web of 11 lines with 260 stations so easy to grasp. Many of the buildings of the Tube and their interiors also have artistic value, and some stations are listed monuments.

In December 1906, the first section of the Piccadilly Line, from Hammersmith in the west to Finsbury Park in the north-east, went into operation. A young architect named Leslie Green was responsible for design matters. His station façades of glazed terracotta tiles in the colour of oxblood, round-arched windows on the upper floor and clearly emphasised cornices are still highly recognisable today. Inside the stations, varied geometric patterns of tiles – white and yellow in Covent Garden, dark green and cream in Gloucester Road – adorn the walls and also serve the purpose of signposting.

In the 1930s, when the line was extended both east and west, the work was entrusted to a second talented architect: Charles Holden, who had already renovated the circular station concourse beneath Piccadilly Circus in 1928, adding the cladding of travertine stone that remains there to this day. He made a study trip to Germany, the Netherlands and Scandinavia to learn about the new Modernist architecture. He then designed stations of simple beauty using a lot of brick and glass, clear outlines, and contrasts between round and angular forms, for example Sudbury Town at the west end of the line and Southgate in the north.

For its 100th anniversary in 2006, the Piccadilly Line was brightened up by contemporary works of art commissioned under the common theme of 'the travels of Marco Polo', and the remaining original tiles were restored in Russell Square and Covent Garden. All of which gives even the most crowded, hot and stuffy Tube journey a certain aesthetic charm.

Address Between Heathrow Airport in the west and Cockfosters in the north | Hours
In central London, the Piccadilly Line runs from approx. 5am to 12.30am and all night on
Fridays and Saturdays | Tip The excellent Museum of London Transport sheds light on
the technology and many other aspects of the Tube – including such design highlights as
historic posters (Piazza of Covent Garden, daily 10am–6pm).

74_Pimlico Road Farmers' Market

Mozart and the magic fruit

At the border of aristocratic Belgravia with Chelsea and Pimlico, the junction of Ebury Street and Pimlico Road forms a little triangular space. Here stands a graceful statue of the young Wolfgang Amadeus Mozart, who composed his first two symphonies in 1764 at the age of nine while living at 180 Ebury Street. As the spot was not built up in those days, Mozart probably had a view of grazing animals and vegetable patches. Nowadays he looks down from his plinth each Saturday on carrots, apples and cabbages when local producers set up their stalls for the farmers' market.

Like other farmers' markets, the scattering of stands on Orange Square displays products that have not travelled any long distance. The aims of offering high-quality foods of known provenance, supporting individual rather than mass-manufactured goods and allowing the customer to meet the producer personally, clearly appeal to the residents of this affluent part of London.

On the triangle of ground beneath Mozart's gaze – it has no official name, but is usually called Orange Square – they find a rich mix of vendors whose offerings go far beyond fruit, vegetables and meat from their own farms. The fish stall sells the catch of the day from a boat on the south coast. Other stands are piled high with fresh pasta and many kinds of pesto, home-baked cake and a great variety of bread, locally made but inspired by France, Italy and Germany. The range of cheese runs from goat's cheese to mature Cheddar and lesser-known products from artisan dairies. The market furnishes everything for a good dinner, which might start with oysters or East Anglian crab meat and be washed down healthily with single-variety pear juice from Kentish orchards. The flower stall provides table decoration.

Address Corner of Pimlico Road, Bourne Street and Ebury Street, SW1W 8NE | **Getting there** Tube to Sloane Square (Circle, District Line) | **Hours** Sat 9am – 2pm | **Tip** A shopping tour in this district could take in the John Lewis department store on Sloane Square and the expensive temptations of King's Road. For information about 20 farmers' markets in London, see www.lfm.org.uk.

75 Postman's Park

A memorial for unsung heroes

After a few days sightseeing in London, you can get tired of monuments. On all sides, military heroes and empire-builders look down with a firm gaze from their plinths, and kings who deserve to be forgotten are honoured with statues. For the democratically minded visitor, a small garden near St Paul's Cathedral makes a refreshing change from this.

The artist George Frederic Watts (1817–1904) had been campaigning for a monument to unknown heroes for 30 years before his plan was fulfilled in July 1900. The first proposal for a site, Hyde Park, was rejected, and finally a decision was made in favour of a small green space laid out in 1880 on the site of an old cemetery. It was called Postman's Park because workers from the nearby General Post Office liked to spend their lunchtime there.

Watts' 'memorial to heroic self-sacrifice' is a modest shelter built onto a wall with space for 120 tiles in five rows. Hand-painted ceramic plaques tell the story of ordinary people who gave their lives for others. A worker in a sugar refinery suffered fatal burns searching for a colleague after a boiler explosion. A railwayman drowned in the River Lea while trying to save someone who had fallen in. A 17-year-old girl protected a child from a runaway horse but died of her own injuries. One hero prevented the suicide of a 'lunatic woman' at Woolwich and was run over by a train. Another died of exhaustion after rescuing people from the ice on Highgate ponds.

The people commemorated on the first 13 plaques, the beautiful turquoise-coloured tiles in the middle row, were chosen by Watts himself. The great ceramics designer William de Morgan made these tiles. In the 30 years after Watts' death, his widow added a further 40 plaques in blue lettering with floral decoration. The most recent dates from 2009, and two of the five rows are still empty. A relief in the first row honours Watts himself.

P·C·HAROLD FRANK RICKETTS
METROPOLITAN POLICE
DROWNED AT TEIGNMOUTH
WHILST TRYING TO RESCUE
A BOY BATHING AND SEEN ·
TO BE IN DIFFICULTY
11 · SEPT · 1916

P·C·EDWARD
BROWN GREE
METROPOLITA
MANY LIVES WERE
DEVOTION TO D
TERRIBLE EXPLOS
SILVERTOWN ·

ELIZABETH BOXALL
AGED 17 OF BETHNAL GREEN
WHO DIED OF INJURIES RECEIVED
IN TRYING TO SAVE
A CHILD
FROM A RUNAWAY HORSE
JUNE · 20 · 1888 ·

HERBERT PETE
STATIONER'S
WHO WAS DROWN
IN ENDEAVOURI
A MAN FROM D
APRIL 2

FREDERICK ALFRED CROFT
INSPECTOR · AGED 31
SAVED A LUNATIC WOMAN
FROM SUICIDE AT WOOLWICH
ARSENAL STATION · BUT WAS
HIMSELF RUN OVER · BY THE TRAIN
· JAN · 11 · 1878 ·

HARRY
KILBVRN ·
DROWNED I
TO SAVE HIS
AFTER HE
JUST BEEN

Address King Edward Street, EC1A 4EU | Getting there Tube to St Paul's (Central Line) |
Hours Daily 8am–7pm or until dusk | Tip 100 metres away at the corner of Newgate
Street, the site of a bombed-out church, Christchurch Newgate, has been transformed into a
fragrant flower garden.

76 The Princess Diana Memorial Fountain

Splashing around is tolerated

When the landscape artist Kathryn Gustafson presented her proposals for a fountain to commemorate Diana, Princess of Wales, she explained that the work was intended to symbolise Diana's life. And truly, the memorial is beautiful, child-friendly, expensive to maintain, and controversial.

The fountain was opened by the Queen in 2004 in the presence of Diana's ex-husband and her sons William and Harry. Installed on a gentle slope near the southern border of Hyde Park, it is not a fountain in the usual sense, but a double watercourse. From its source at the top, water flows in two directions to the bottom of a large oval, where the streams unite in a basin. The bed of the streams, made from Cornish granite, is between three and six metres wide and 210 metres long. Three bridges, small waterfalls and changes of gradient add variety. Grooves, hollows and curves in the channel make the water dance and play. It foams, gurgles and bubbles, splashes up through little jets and slowly comes to rest as it swirls around the lower basin.

Shortly after its opening, negative publicity muddied the waters. People slipped on the shiny granite, and one child suffered a head injury. In autumn, fallen leaves blocked the channels. The fountain was closed for remedial work, including roughening up the most slippery surfaces. These measures seem to have been successful. In warm weather, the fountain now delights London's children. Adults too roll up their trouser legs and wade gingerly through the channel. Officially, visitors to the park may sit on the edge and dangle their feet in the water, but not walk in the fountain. However, the security staff who are constantly present turn a blind eye while young and old enjoy themselves. Diana would surely have liked it.

Address In the south-west of Hyde Park | **Getting there** Tube to Knightsbridge (Piccadilly Line) | **Hours** Daily from 10am, Apr–Aug until 8pm, Sept until 7pm, Mar, Oct until 6pm, Nov–Feb until 4pm | **Tip** The Diana Memorial Playground, with a pirate ship for children and benches for their parents, is at the north-west corner of Kensington Gardens.

77 The Prospect of Whitby

A last drink for condemned pirates

The Prospect of Whitby is the very embodiment of the notion of a seamen's tavern: the pewter-topped bar is supported by wooden barrels, the posts that hold up the low ceiling were once ships' masts, the uneven stone slabs on the floor date from the 18th century, and the fireplace is black with soot. Diners seated in the Admiral's Cabin, which has the appearance of a salon in a battleship from Horatio Nelson's day, have a view of the river through lattice windows, while those who take their glasses into the beer garden to drink a pint beneath the willow tree look out on passing boats – and a gallows with a dangling noose.

The gallows, although not genuine, is a reminder of true stories. 500 years ago, an inn called The Pelican, later known as The Devil's Tavern, stood on this site. It is reported that the adventurer Sir Hugh Willoughby spent his last evening ashore here in 1533 before sailing round the North Cape to look for the North-East Passage to China. With his entire crew, he froze to death on the Kola Peninsula. He was not the only man destined to die who took a last drink here by the Thames. Just a little way upstream – the exact spot is not known – was Execution Dock, where pirates were hanged.

Punishing crime on the high seas, for example mutiny and piracy, was the responsibility of the Admiralty, which however had no jurisdiction on land. The gallows was therefore set up in the river, close to the bank but in a place where it stood in water even at low tide. Condemned men were taken there in a cart and given a quart of ale before they were strung up. The last to suffer this fate were two sailors who murdered their captain in 1830. Corpses were left on the gallows until the tide had covered their heads three times. In some exceptional cases such as that of the notorious pirate Captain Kidd in 1701, the body of the felon was displayed in a cage for years. The tavern was also a haunt of the "Hanging Judge" Jeffries in the 1680s.

Address 57 Wapping Wall, E1W 3SH | Getting there Overground to Wapping (East London Line) | Hours Daily noon–11pm | Tip The Town of Ramsgate (62 Wapping High Street), which also has a pleasant riverside beer garden, is another authentically old pub. Next to it, Wapping Old Stairs lead down to the shore of the Thames.

78 Quantum Cloud
Art beneath wide skies

London is densely built in spite of its extensive parks. In the City, skyscrapers stand close to the noisy streets, and in the West End, the pavements are constantly crowded. Yet if you long for wide skies and a distant horizon, solitude lies only 13 minutes from Westminster by Jubilee Line, at the tip of the Greenwich peninsula. The Thames is wider here than in the city centre. Gulls screech, waves slap on the embankment, and the ebbing tide reveals sandy beaches. No buildings block the view across the water.

A little distance from North Greenwich Pier, a sculpture rises 30 metres into the air: a 'cloud'. At its centre, a human shape can be discerned. Conversations with a physicist inspired Antony Gormley to create this work. Much of his art is concerned with the relationship of the human body to space and matter. On the beach at Crosby north of Liverpool he placed 100 iron casts of his own body, scattered across the sand to be covered as the tide comes in. In 2007 he installed 31 male figures on the roofs of buildings along the South Bank in London. His most famous work remains the huge Angel of the North in Gateshead. Gormley constructed Quantum Cloud from angular steel rods with the outline of a tetrahedron that cluster loosely around the human form in their midst. Their position around the body was determined by random generation.

This airy, diffuse shape contrasts with a massive presence behind the observer: the O2 arena, the former Millennium Dome. Things are happening in North Greenwich. The so-called Emirates Air Line, a cable-car, takes passengers across the river to the Roy al Docks at a height of 90 metres. Housing is being built on a large scale on industrial wasteland. Solitude will be less easy to find in North Greenwich, but by the riverside the feeling of wide open space will remain. The Thames Path shows the way east to the Thames Barrier, then to the estuary and the sea.

Address Bank of the Thames near North Greenwich Pier, SE10 London | Getting there
Tube to North Greenwich (Jubilee Line) | Tip A few hundred metres west of *Quantum Cloud*, also on the river, is a work of art called *Slice of Reality*: Richard Wilson cut a slice out of the middle of a cargo ship and left it for the current and waves to do their work.

79 The Queen Mother Memorial

Horses, corgis and the Blitz

Among London's monuments to royalty, one stands out for its personal representation of the subject's character and tastes. The bronze reliefs in question are part of the King George VI & Queen Elizabeth Memorial, as the ensemble is officially called. In part, it is highly conventional: George VI, wearing Royal Navy uniform, stands high on his plinth. In front of him, placed lower down, is the statue of his wife and queen, dressed in finery that includes a large feathered hat. However, on the wall between these two figures the life of the Queen Mother is presented in a very different style. The memorial is positioned on the north side of The Mall near Clarence House, which was her residence from 1953 until she died in 2002 at the age of 101.

Born Elizabeth Bowes-Lyon, the daughter of Scottish aristocrats, in 1923 she married the second son of George V, who became king in 1936, following the abdication of his elder brother. As Queen Elizabeth, she earned recognition for supporting her shy husband, who took on the unwanted burden of kingship, and died in 1952, leaving her a widow for the following 50 years. One relief depicts the royal couple with their two daughters, and shows Elizabeth talking to bombed-out residents of the East End during the Second World War. She and George VI refused to be evacuated to safety in Canada. When bombs hit Buckingham Palace, Queen Elizabeth said: 'I'm glad … it makes me feel I can look the East End in the face.'

The other relief is devoted to the Queen Mother's passions: horse races and corgi dogs. On 4 August, 2000, a parade was held for her 100th birthday, and in April 2002 millions watched her funeral procession. Critics of the monarchy point to the extravagance of her lifestyle, but she performed public duties right up to the year of her death, and was loved by the British people.

Address The Mall, SW1Y 5DG – north side, halfway between Trafalgar Square and Buckingham Palace | Getting there Tube to Green Park (Piccadilly, Victoria, Jubilee Line), or St James's Park (District, Circle Line) | Tip Each August, Clarence House is open to the public, giving an opportunity to admire fine furnishings, art and the garden (www.rct.uk/visit).

80___Queen Square

A green place for parents, children and queens

Who is the queen of Queen Square? The statue cast from lead in the gardens at its centre was long thought to represent Queen Anne (reigned 1702–1714). The square, laid out in 1716, was named after Anne, but the figure probably represents Charlotte of Mecklenburg-Strelitz (1744–1818), King George III's queen. Her interest in botany is commemorated in the name of an exotic bloom, the strelitzia. Although Charlotte and George did not meet each other until their wedding day, they had a happy marriage. She bore 15 children and he, in a radical break with royal tradition, never took a mistress. The physician who treated George III in his later years of mental illness lived on Queen Square. It was decided that the King should live in his doctor's house for a time, and Charlotte is said to have rented the cellar of the house at no. 1 as a store for her husband's favourite food. Today, this building is a pub called The Queen's Larder.

Whether Anne or Charlotte, the statue is magnificent. It depicts a person of dainty stature with a resolute expression and curly, shoulder-length hair, wearing a crown and an opulent dress with a plunging neckline, a floral pattern and tassels suspended from the girdle. Her outstretched right hand once held a sceptre. One more queen is honoured on the square. In 1977, for the silver jubilee of Elizabeth II, a basin of flowers was placed at the other end of the gardens. Slabs on the ground in front and behind bear verses by Philip Larkin and Ted Hughes.

A more recent work of art on Queen Square shows a mother with baby in the middle of the gardens, which have been open to the public since 1999. They are much visited by young patients and their parents from the nearby children's hospital in Great Ormond Street. The square with its rose beds and flowering shrubs gives them a quiet place to sit when times are difficult.

Address Bloomsbury, west of Russell Square, WC1N 3AQ | Getting there Tube to Russell Square (Piccadilly Line) | Hours Garden: during daylight hours | Tip The café in the Mary Ward Centre at the south end of Queen Square serves reasonably priced vegetarian dishes (Mon–Fri 10am–4pm during university term-time).

81 Richmond-on-Thames
Where the river takes on a rural character

Of all the structures that span the Thames within the boundaries of London, Richmond Bridge, opened in 1777, is the oldest and, with its graceful stone arches, one of the most beautiful. It is a starting point for lovely riverside walks. Towards the city centre, the path goes through the historic Old Deer Park to the Royal Botanical Gardens in Kew. On sunny days, the area to the south of the bridge presents a carefree scene of children feeding ducks and swans. Cyclists and walkers find an array of attractive cafés and pubs with outdoor tables. Rowing boats can be hired, and river steamers take trippers upstream to Hampton Court Palace and downstream to Westminster.

Although this pleasant small-town atmosphere provides a foretaste of the rural charms of the Thames valley further west and gives the impression of being a great distance from the sea, this is in fact still a tidal stretch of the river. The tide reaches Richmond about 45 minutes later than London Bridge and moves a few miles further upstream to Teddington – more than 50 river miles from the estuary.

For a famous view of the Thames valley, leave the riverside at Richmond and ascend Richmond Hill along the road of the same name. The purchasers of houses on this road have acquired a fine prospect from their upper windows and made a rock-solid investment. One of them is Pete Townshend of The Who, who bought The Wick (halfway up on the left) from Ronnie Wood of the Rolling Stones. The neighbouring Wick House was built in about 1770 for the painter Sir Joshua Reynolds, first president of the Royal Academy. Down to the right are the well-tended flower beds of Terrace Gardens, from where it is not far to the highest point on Richmond Hill. Reynolds and Turner painted the view towards Windsor, which is as impressive today as it was in their time: meadows, trees, and the shining silver Thames.

Address Richmond-on-Thames, TW9 | Getting there Tube to Richmond (District Line) |
Tip Tide Tables under the arches of Richmond Bridge with its outdoor terrace is a
recommended café. Up the hill, The Roebuck (130 Richmond Hill) is a traditional pub with
a great view from the beer garden.

82 __ Robbie Williams' House
Disharmony among musicians

The grand residences on Melbury Road in Kensington were built as an artists' colony in the 19th century. Two of them belong to musicians today. In 2013, Robbie Williams paid £17.5 million for Woodland House (number 31), a property with tall brick chimneys, white balcony balustrades and 47 rooms. His neighbour, Led Zeppelin guitarist Jimmy Page, moved into Tower House (number 29) back in 1972, having offered a higher price than the other bidder – David Bowie. Page was on friendly terms with Williams' predecessor in Woodland House, the film director Michael Winner. However, the neighbourly harmony came to an end when Williams applied for permission to build a two-storey subterranean extension with a nine-metre swimming pool.

Page was concerned about the stability and fragile interior decoration of Tower House. With its asymmetrical façade and round stair turret, it was designed by William Burges, a major figure of 19th-century Gothic Revival art and architecture. For Burges, the house was both a home and a kind of showroom, where he displayed to clients the beauty of the stained-glass windows, mosaics, murals and wood carvings that adorn it. The conservation authority Historic England gave a grade-one listing to these 'important interiors'. Jimmy Page sees himself as the guardian of a precious gem. To avoid harmful vibrations, at home he plays only acoustic, never electric guitar.

The neighbours waged war on each other through the media, with Williams disparaging Page on the radio. A letter to the local council from a resident of the street accused Williams of deliberately provoking Page by blasting the music of Page's old rivals, Black Sabbath, Pink Floyd and Deep Purple, at full volume from his window. In 2018, Williams gained the planning permission he sought, but with instructions to limit any noise and reverberations from the building work.

Address 31 Melbury Road, W14 8AB | Getting there Tube to High Street Kensington (District, Circle Line), then a 10-minute walk west along the High Street and right into Melbury Road | Tip Around the corner at number 12 Holland Park Road, the home of the artist Lord Leighton (1830–1896) was designed in an exuberant Moorish style, and furnished with mosaics, Islamic tiles and Leighton's paintings (Wed–Mon 10am–5.30pm, www.rbkc.gov.uk).

83__ The Rolling Bridge

A party piece by a celebrated designer

The developers of shiny new Merchant Square around the canal basin near Paddington Station wanted to add something special to the usual offices, homes, bars and restaurants at such sites – a striking feature, a talking point. The Rolling Bridge, invented by Heatherwick Studio, implemented this plan in 2004. Thomas Heatherwick, born in London in 1970, is known for the originality of his designs of a wide array of products and buildings. They include the British pavilion at Expo 2010 in Shanghai, with an exterior that looked like a dandelion seed-head, the new generation of red double-decker buses for London, and the curving roof of Coal Drops Yard in King's Cross.

For the canal in Paddington, Heatherwick Studio came up with a moving bridge – but not a conventional drawbridge or swing bridge. This one curls up like a caterpillar by means of hydraulic power. The 12-metre bridge of steel and wood consists of eight triangular segments. In the open position, the segments lie level in a row, spanning a short section of water. At the touch of a button, one end of the bridge rises and arcs towards the other end until it has rolled up completely, coming to rest as an octagon. This mechanism is regularly demonstrated to an admiring audience.

At the east end of the basin is another innovative moving bridge. The Fan Bridge, designed by Knight Architects, is made up of five parallel 20-metre arms that form the surface for walking. At one end the arms are firmly anchored, whereas on the other side of the water they rest upon the bank. The mechanism raises them diagonally. They pivot upwards at different angles, opening like a fan until the uppermost arm is poised at 80 degrees to the surface of the canal. Neither of the bridges opens frequently to let boats pass, because Merchant Square is at the end of the canal. It's all about the spectacle!

Address Merchant Square, W2 1NW – north of Praed Street, which runs between the main entrance to Paddington Station and Edgware Road | **Getting there** Tube to Paddington or Edgware Road (several lines) | **Hours** Check www.merchantsquare.co.uk/bridges for demonstration times; normally Wed, Fri at noon, Sat 2pm | **Tip** Motorboats can be hired at Merchant Square to chug slowly along the canal to Little Venice and Regent's Park (www.goboat.co.uk).

84_ The Roman City Wall

Londinium has not quite disappeared

London's ancient defences are not conspicuous, although their position is still recognisable on the map in the names of streets such as London Wall and Houndsditch. You can walk around the City for a long time without noticing them, and then unexpectedly chance upon a high wall of rough stonework.

The first Roman trading post on the site that is now the City of London was not protected by a wall. This made it easier for the tribal queen Boudicca to burn Londinium to the ground in AD 60. The three-mile-long, six-metre-high Roman wall was probably not constructed until around the year 200; 85,000 tons of stone were transported from Kent for the purpose. Six city gates were the starting points for roads that led to all parts of the province of Britannia. Through periods of decay and rebuilding, most of the wall that encircled the Roman settlement stood for over 1,500 years. In the Middle Ages a further gate was built. Towers, parapets and walkways were added, but the basis of the defences was still the Roman wall. The gates were rebuilt again and again, then demolished in 1760 in order to widen the roads.

In the south-east corner of the fortified area, where William the Conqueror built the Tower, an imposing stretch of the old wall still stands. The Roman stonework stands to a height of 4.40 metres here. The two metres at the top date from the Middle Ages. Originally, the rubble core of the wall was clad with smooth-faced masonry, interspersed with layers of red tiles for stability, but the good-looking stones of the outer shell were plundered and re-used elsewhere over the centuries, leaving the wall with its present rough appearance. In this spot by the Tower, a little garden with a statue of Emperor Trajan lends dignity to the remains. More stretches of wall, including bastions and a moat, can be seen in the Barbican and near the Museum of London.

Address Tower Hill, EC3N 4AB | Getting there Tube to Tower Hill (Circle, District Line) | Tip Excellent exhibitions in the Museum of London bring Roman Londinium back to life (London Wall, daily 10am – 6pm, www.museumoflondon.org.uk).

85 The Roof Garden

Flowers and concrete

The South Bank cultural quarter is usually a hive of activity. Here, the Queen Elizabeth Hall opened in 1967 as a stage for classical music and dance, and now electronic music and other genres. The other institutions of the Southbank Centre are the more intimate Purcell Room for chamber music, the National Theatre, the Hayward Gallery, the Royal Festival Hall, the National Poetry Library, and the BFI arthouse cinema. While there's no doubt this ensemble is a cultural gem, opinions differ regarding its architecture. Fans of brutalism love it, and for skateboarders the concrete surfaces make an ideal arena for practising stunts. Countless pedestrians, both tourists and Londoners, pass by the chunky, angular structures on the Thames-side path between Westminster Bridge and Tower Bridge every day.

To get away from the bustle, look upwards. Amongst the grey concrete walls, canary-yellow steps ascend to the roof garden of the Queen Elizabeth Hall. On all sides, raised beds are filled with a profusion of flowering plants: yellow marigolds, red-hot pokers, as well as wildflowers such as white yarrow and blue chicory. In summer, the scent of sweet peas fills the air, and fruit trees and shrubs flourish against a background of raw concrete. Visitors can order drinks and snacks from a hut and sit at a scattering of tables, some of them repurposed cable drums and wooden barrels.

The garden is tended by a project called Grounded EcoTherapy, which offers horticultural work as therapy for people affected by homelessness, addiction and mental illness. They have a meaningful task here, get a visible, blooming reward for their efforts, and gain confidence to enter or re-enter paid employment. The garden was created in 2011 to mark the 60th anniversary of the Festival of Britain, which brightened up the grey post-war years with culture and entertainment.

Address South Bank Centre, SE1 8XX | Getting there Tube to Waterloo (Northern, Bakerloo, Jubilee Line), or Embankment (District, Circle, Northern Line) and cross the Thames | Hours Apr–Jun, Sept, Oct noon–9pm, Jul & Aug 10am–10.30pm | Tip Visitors to the South Bank Food Market next to the Queen Elizabeth Hall can enjoy street food from around the world and buy freshly baked goods to take home (Fri noon–8pm, Sat 11am–8pm, Sun noon–6pm).

86 The Ropewalk

Street food from the railway arches

Bermondsey, once an industrial district, has not shaken off its working-class character, but it is changing. Although the wide railway viaduct that has sliced through the area since 1839 is anything but pretty, its miles of brick arches are useful – for storage space or car repair shops, and in recent years for producing, cooking and serving interesting food. An alley next to the tracks has become trendy for street food at weekends. Some of the stalls are run by chefs and producers who once supplied the better-known Borough Market but were looking for a smaller, more upmarket event. The official name is Maltby Street Market, but the stalls are in The Ropewalk, a strip of land where ropes were once made. Around 25 stands line one side of the alley, and further eateries occupy the deep railway arches on the other side.

The organisers' stated aim is to offer quality and variety. The aromas of Ethiopia, Lebanon and Morocco waft on the air. Venezuelan arepas are made from white corn flour with various fillings. Europe is represented by Greek mezes and Sicilian arancini. British treats are also on offer, for example excellent beefsteaks and oysters from Maldon. Given that porridge and Scotch eggs were taken upmarket for foodies long ago, fans of those staples of down-to-earth home or pub catering need not go hungry. And no one who sticks to a vegan, gluten-free or lactose-free diet will feel discriminated against. There are also indulgences such as hot waffles and calorie-rich brownies.

As for beverages, healthy options such as vegetable juice are sold alongside alcoholic drinks that are as hip as the Londoners who come here: craft beer and cider are made in microbreweries in the brick arches, the Little Bird gin distillery serves its creative cocktails, and the flavours of Spain are on offer at the Bodega Tozino, which serves jamón to accompany its wines.

Address Ropewalk, between Maltby Street and Millstream Road, SE1 3PA, www.maltby.st | **Getting there** From London Bridge Station walk parallel to the viaduct along St Thomas Street, then follow Crucifix Lane and Druid Street to Tanner Street, and pass under the bridge to Maltby Street | **Hours** Sat 10am–5pm, Sun 11am–4pm | **Tip** Little more than a five-minute walk away is a gallery renowned for contemporary art: the White Cube Gallery at 144 Bermondsey Street (from Maltby Street via Tanner Street, www.whitecube.com).

87 Royal Arcade

Connections to the palace are good for business

When 'The Arcade' opened in 1879, linking Bond Street with Albemarle Street in the high-class district of Mayfair, the idea of putting a row of shops beneath a single roof was not new. Covered passageways like this had been built in Paris almost 100 years earlier, and the English weather was an excellent reason for copying the plan. London's oldest arcade is the beautiful, though now sadly neglected, Royal Opera Arcade on Haymarket, which dates from 1816. Three years later Burlington Arcade appeared on Piccadilly at the south end of Mayfair.

When it was inaugurated, The Arcade was not yet entitled to call itself 'royal', despite the richness of its architecture. Its classical façades have elaborate plaster adornments. Shoppers who care to take their eyes off the luxury goods and look up are greeted by lightly clad goddesses and their attendants, mythological scenes representing Prosperity and Plenty. The decorative details are picked out in white, orange and apricot. The view along the interior of the arcade is a lovely perspective of round arches. Heavy lamps hang beneath the glass roof, and the large shop windows are framed in dark polished wood.

A shirt maker who had the warrant to supply the court of Queen Victoria gained the epithet 'royal' for the arcade. A royal florist and a supplier of heraldic stationery were also present. Today, the products sold here are as fine as ever. They range from the fragrances of an exclusive perfumery to made-to-measure shoes, works of art and silverware for high-society dinner tables. A holder of a royal warrant is still represented: the chocolatier Charbonnel et Walker, maker of a drinking chocolate that the Mayfair clientele pronounces to be divine. Does Buckingham Palace order chocolate truffles for guests of state and evenings around the television, or cocoa for a warming bedtime drink? That, of course, is confidential.

Address 28 Old Bond Street, W1S 4SL | **Getting there** Tube to Green Park (Jubilee, Piccadilly, Victoria Line) | **Tip** Mayfair is not only about luxury consumption. Handel & Hendrix in London (25 Brook Street, for hours see handelhendrix.org) was once the dwelling of the composer George Frideric Handel. Some 200 years later, Jimi Hendrix lived next door.

88 The Scalpel

Play video!

If you walk along the south bank of the Thames close to Tower Bridge on a sunny day and take photographs of the high-rise office blocks across the river, you might get a surprise when looking at the images later: 'What, did I take a video by mistake?' The triangular 'Play' symbol has appeared on the screen. But no, this is a trick of the light: the sun has been reflected in the sloping roof of an angular glass skyscraper and, depending where you stand on the river bank, the bright sunlight can form the shape of a horizontal isosceles triangle.

The sharp-edged architecture of this conspicuous building has given it the nickname 'The Scalpel' – 'London's sharpest landmark', according to the marketing slogan. The owners of The Shard might disagree, as their 310-metre glass prism is even more razor-like than The Scalpel, whose 38 storeys rise no higher than a modest 190 metres. This is the work of the American architectural practice Kohn Pedersen Fox, which has designed skyscrapers all over the world. The client that commissioned The Scalpel, the insurance company Berkley, has moved its European headquarters into the acres of office space.

When the towers of the City of London shot into the sky in the early 21st century, the trend of giving them memorable nicknames began too. The fun started in 2004 with the circular 'Gherkin' (officially St Mary Axe). Ten years later, the sloping south front of The Leadenhall Building inevitably earned its fitting moniker 'The Cheesegrater'. Soon afterwards, 20 Fenchurch Street spread out at the top instead of narrowing, as a result of which it was christened 'The Walkie-Talkie'. It remains to be seen whether more bold new shapes will be built. Planning permission was refused for a Tulip Tower, and the combined effects of Brexit and the COVID-19 pandemic may put the brakes on any construction boom.

Address 52 Lime Street, at the corner of Leadenhall Street, EC3M 7AW,
www.thescalpelec3.co.uk | Getting there DLR or Tube to Bank (Central, Northern,
Waterloo & City Line), then along Cornhill and Leadenhall Street, or Monument Station,
and follow Gracechurch Street to Leadenhall Street | Tip Kohn Pedersen Fox also designed
110 Bishopsgate, where diners in the restaurants on floors 38–40, Duck and Waffle
(www.duckandwaffle.com) and Sushi Samba (www.sushisamba.com), have stunning views.

89　Shad Thames

Sought-after homes in Charles Dickens' slum

The works of Charles Dickens contain powerful passages about life in the poor quarters of 19th-century London. The south bank of the Thames east of Tower Bridge (then not yet built) was known to the novelist from visits that he made in the company of the river police. In *Oliver Twist*, he described the houses around St Saviour's Dock as follows: 'rooms so small, so filthy, so confined, that the air would seem to be too tainted even for the dirt and squalor which they shelter; wooden chambers thrusting themselves out above the mud and threatening to fall into it ... every loathsome indication of filth, rot, and garbage.'

Since then the scene has changed twice. The homes in Shad Thames, a street that runs parallel to the river as far as St Saviour's Dock, are now apartments in converted warehouses and shiny new buildings with a river view. Many residents are employed in the financial sector and take a short trip across Tower Bridge to reach the office. Expensive bars and restaurants around Shad Thames help them to spend their money. In 1873, three years after the death of Dickens, huge warehouses for tea, coffee, spices and grain were built here. The last of them was closed in 1972, and redevelopment began in the 1980s. The walkways that criss-cross Shad Thames high above street level, once connecting storage spaces on either side of the road, are now the balconies of flats. The names of the residential blocks – Vanilla Court, Cayenne Court, Tea Trade Wharf – are reminders of the old use of the buildings.

At St Saviour's Dock too, where a subterranean river, the Neckinger, flows into the Thames, warehouses have become fashionable apartments. In 2008, a campaigning environmental group cleaned up the narrow waterway where Dickens staged the dramatic death of the villain Bill Sikes and his vicious bulldog, which expired pitifully in the stinking slime.

Address South bank of the Thames east of Tower Bridge, SE1 2YD | Getting there Tube to Tower Hill (Circle, District Line) | Tip The Fashion and Textile Museum founded by Zandra Rhodes is close by: 83 Bermondsey Street, Tue–Sat 11am–6pm.

90 _ Shoreditch Street Art

Legal or illegal, subversive or sponsored

The transformation of Shoreditch from run-down to hip began in the 1980s, when artists set up studios in vacant commercial properties. Cool bars and nightclubs followed in their wake, and start-ups from the IT sector clustered around Old Street. As rents rose in the new millennium, many artists moved further east, and in recent years sleek new buildings have appeared. For the time being, Shoreditch remains a zone of transition between the City and points east, a place of galleries, unconventional designer shops and creative street art.

To the east of Shoreditch High Street, artists from all over the world have made their mark on walls and doors. On some streets, almost every available space has been pasted, painted freehand, sprayed using templates or adorned with little sculptures. Internationally known street artists have worked here: Banksy inevitably, Space Invader and Roa, who paints outsized animals – in Shoreditch a bird four storeys high. Some operate with the permission of the house owners, others illegally. Some studied at art school, others emerged self-taught from the graffiti scene. Some are sponsored by galleries that use attention-grabbing street art as publicity for their exhibitions, others oppose the art business on principle. One sprayer receives a lucrative commission, another is summoned for a court appearance.

Street art is a wildly creative cosmos of humorous, political or poetic work that is constantly renewed. Some works are quickly ruined by tags and low-grade graffiti, then painted over within a few weeks. The painting on the right, juxtaposing a British ultra-nationalist with a Muslim preacher of hate, has already disappeared. Work by respected artists may stay untouched for a long time, or even be repaired by supporters if it is defaced. And when all of Shoreditch becomes chic, street art will enliven another part of London.

Address Between Shoreditch High Street and Brick Lane, E1 | **Getting there** Tube to Liverpool Street (Central, Circle, Hammersmith & City, Metropolitan Line) | **Tip** Not hip, but never out of fashion: excellent traditional fish and chips at Poppies (6–8 Hanbury Street, Sun–Wed 11am–10pm, Thu–Sat 11am–11pm).

91 Shri Swaminarayan Mandir

A Hindu temple, open to everyone

In Neasden, of all places, often mocked as the epitome of a face-less suburb and described by Sir John Betjeman as the 'home of the gnome and the average citizen', a gleaming white apparition rises above the rows of semi-detached houses as if transplanted from a fairy tale. A Hindu spiritual organisation, the Swaminarayan group, found cheap building land here – but otherwise spared no expense. Over a three-year period up to 1995, volunteers under expert super-vision built a 60-metre- long temple with domes and sugarloaf tow-ers using Bulgarian limestone and 1,200 tons of Carrara marble. The architecture is based on Vedic texts and used no structural steel. The stone was carved in India by 1,400 sculptors trained in depicting the world of Hindu gods, then shipped to London.

The result is breathtaking. Almost every surface is elaborately carved with swirling, snaking patterns and adorned by deities. Visi-tors arriving at the main entrance are greeted by dancers waving their stone limbs between deeply incised columns. The interior is almost more sumptuous than the outside. From lobbies whose ceilings are covered in wood carvings, the stairway leads up to the Great Hall, where an 'arti' ceremony is performed every day at 11.45am in a brightly illuminated space under a dome supported by marble col-umns and adorned with depictions of the Hindu gods.

Those who attend are expected to take off their shoes and dress modestly. Non-Hindus are welcomed sincerely to the ceremony, in which monks perform movements with burning candles in their hands in front of gaudily dressed images of gods to the sound of drums and bells. When this ends, worshippers put their hands to the candles and spread the divine power of the flame over their heads. After the ceremony, visitors can walk out onto a balcony for a close-up view of the temple sculptures and view an exhibition about Hinduism. It is an uplifting experience in an unexpected location.

Address 105–119 Brentfield Road, Neasden, NW10 8LD, www.londonmandir.baps.org |
Getting there Tube to Stonebridge Park (Bakerloo Line), then 15 minutes' walk (sign-posted) | Hours Daily 9am–6pm, for times of ceremonies see website | Tip Next to the car park opposite the temple, the Shayona Restaurant serves excellent vegetarian Indian meals at very reasonable prices (daily noon–10pm, +44 (0)20 8965 3365).

92 __ Spencer House
Old money, expensive taste

'Historic property in prime location, eight reception rooms (some renovation required), view of Green Park'. The agent's ad was not needed when the eighth Earl Spencer let his house near Buckingham Palace to Lord Jacob Rothschild's investment company in 1985 on a 120-year lease. The Spencers had not lived in their townhouse since 1926. In 1942, as a precaution against bombing, the furniture and many fittings were removed to their country seat. More than four decades later, Rothschild's company commenced an exemplary and breathtakingly expensive restoration of the building, which had been used for offices.

Spencer House was built from 1756 for the first earl by John Vardy in the Palladian style. The magnificence of Vardy's interiors on the ground floor increases on a circuit from the library and the dining room with its view of the park to the exuberantly decorated Palm Room, where gilded columns in the shape of palm trees frame a domed space in which a copy of the Venus de' Medici is the centrepiece. The highlight of the first floor, designed by James 'Athenian' Stuart according to ancient Roman models, is the Painted Room, with frescoes on the theme of love for the happily married young earl.

During restoration work, copies were made of the original carved door cases and skirting boards, as well as six superb marble fireplaces (at 10,000 man-hours each), and 40,000 pieces of gold leaf made the Palm Room gleam again. With the help of loans such as paintings from the Royal Collection and furniture from the V & A Museum, interiors as sumptuous as any in London regained their original appearance. At the insistence of the lenders, the house is open to the public on some Sundays. On other days of the week, London's most exclusive event location is rented out at dizzying prices – during the Olympic Games in 2012 to the International Olympic Committee.

Address 27 St James's Place, SW1A 1NR | Getting there Tube to Green Park (Jubilee, Piccadilly, Victoria Line) | Hours Sun except Aug, reservation at www.spencerhouse.co.uk | Tip The daughter of the eighth Earl Spencer was Diana, Princess of Wales. The home of her parents-in-law is open to visitors in July, August and September (Buckingham Palace, daily from 9.30am, last admission 4.15pm, www.rct.uk).

93__St Anne's Church, Soho

Where the German king of Corsica is buried

From Wardour Street, steps lead up to a garden by the tower of St Anne's Church. This former cemetery is a good two metres above road level, raised by the mortal remains of 60,000 people who were buried here in the 150 years before it closed in 1853 – 60,000 life stories, surely none of them more curious than that of Theodor von Neuhoff.

Born to a noble Westphalian family in 1694, Neuhoff was an agent for the kings of Spain and Sweden. He made a fortune in Paris through financial speculation, but had to flee from the city twice after running up gambling debts, and in 1736 became the leader of Corsican separatists who wanted to liberate their island from Genoese rule. They elected him their king, but the plan to invade Corsica failed. After further adventures, Neuhoff ended up in a debtors' prison in London, allegedly gained his release by pledging the kingdom to his creditors, then subsisted until his death in 1756 on the charity of prominent persons. One of them, Horace Walpole, composed the lines that can still be read on the tower of St Anne's:

The grave, great teacher, to a level brings
Heroes and beggars, galley slaves and kings.
But Theodore this moral learned ere dead:
Fate poured its lessons on his living head,
Bestowed a kingdom, but denied him bread.

Bombs destroyed the church in September 1940. The top of the surviving tower is an oddity that an architectural historian described as 'two crossed beer barrels'. On open days, visitors can climb up to see the bell, dating from the foundation of the church in 1686, and the clock mechanism. From premises on Dean Street, the parish of St Anne's does valuable work for drug addicts and the homeless. The old south entrance to the church on Shaftesbury Avenue is now a souvenir shop.

Address Wardour Street, near Shaftesbury Avenue, W1D 6HT | Getting there Tube to Leicester Square (Piccadilly, Northern Line) | Hours Garden daily 10am until dusk | Tip The justly admired chef Yotam Ottolenghi has a restaurant in Soho: Nopi, 59 Wells Street, +44 (0)20/39638270, ottolenghi.co.uk.

94 St Bartholomew-the-Great

The court jester's church, now a film set

St Bartholomew-the-Great bears the marks of its 900-year history. Rahere, a canon of St Paul's Cathedral who is reported to have once been a minstrel or fool at the court of King Henry I, founded an Augustinian priory in 1123 outside the city walls, next to an open space called Smithfield. This was the place where knights engaged in battle in tournaments, and also a livestock market, where William Wallace was executed and Protestants burned in the 16th century.

In its present form, "St Barts" is a rare example in London of the Norman style of architecture, but only the east end of Rahere's church building remains. When the priory was dissolved in 1539, the nave was demolished and its ground used as a churchyard. One of the doorways from the west end of the church remains. With the addition of a half-timbered structure above the old entrance, it now serves as a gatehouse. The church was spared in the Great Fire of 1666. A thorough restoration in the 19th century removed cow sheds and workshops that had been added. One wing of the cloister is still intact as a reminder of Rahere's original purpose, and the founder's tomb inside the church shows him in the garb of the Augustinian order.

Tiers of round-headed arches and contrasts of light and shade have a powerful impact inside. Light streams through the clear-glazed upper windows, and the aisles beneath are dark tunnels. After Sunday service, clouds of incense rise through slanting rays of sunlight in this ancient, hallowed space. No wonder film directors love St Barts, and have made it the setting for scenes in *Four Weddings and a Funeral*, *Shakespeare in Love* and *Sherlock Holmes*. It's no surprise to learn that a ghost – a monk looking for a lost sandal – stalks the gloomy passages. At night, the smell of burning flesh is said to waft over from Smithfield, where heretics died at the stake.

Address Cloth Market, EC1A 9DS | Getting there Tube to St Paul's (Central Line) |
Hours Mon–Fri 8.30am–4pm, Sat 10.30am–4pm, Sun 8.30am–8pm | Tip Smithfield
meat market is the only historic wholesale market still operating in the City; it's best to
visit early in the morning, but its architecture in wrought-iron and glass, built in 1868, is
worth a look at any time.

95 St Bride's

Slender steeple, creepy crypt

The graceful tower of St Bride's Church is often said to have been the model for wedding cakes. A close look raises doubts about this. The tower and steeple, 71 metres high, consist of a square base, five octagonal storeys, and an obelisk at the top. Even if a baker succeeded in copying this slender, complex construction, the proportion of icing sugar would be far too high to make an edible cake.

St Bride's is one of the most admired works of Sir Christopher Wren. Its magnificent interior was reconstructed following damage by fire bombs which left only the outer walls and the tower standing in December 1940. Restoration, which renewed the masterly wood carving on the altar and choir stalls, gilded rosettes and marble floor, was supported by newspaper magnates, as St Bride's lies just off Fleet Street and has been associated with the press for 500 years. One of London's first printers, Wynkyn de Worde, worked next to the church in around 1500, and was buried in St Bride's.

Wren's church of 1675 had six predecessors. There is a tradition that the first of them was founded in the 6th century by the Irish St Bride, also known as St Bridget of Kildare, herself. Alternatively it may have been built by Celtic monks who revered her. Before that, a Roman house occupied the site. In 1210 Parliament met in the church. The diarist Samuel Pepys was baptised here, and the poet Milton belonged to the parish. Traces of many periods can be seen in the crypt, where excavations revealed forgotten burial vaults, one packed to the roof with 300 skeletons, and another containing bones and skulls carefully arranged in a chequerboard pattern. Among the items in the exhibition below the church is a patented iron coffin that was designed to foil body snatchers. Until 1832, public executions were the only legal source of bodies for dissection, so the requirements of the medical profession for experiments and teaching had to be met by a gruesome trade in stolen corpses.

Address Fleet Street, near Ludgate Circus, EC4Y 8AU | Getting there Tube to
Blackfriars (Circle, District Line) | Hours Mon–Fri 8am–6pm, Sat 10am–3.30pm,
Sun 10am–6.30pm; guided tours: Tue 2.15pm | Tip An outstanding choir consisting of
12 professional singers can be heard during church services twice each Sunday (for the
programme, see www.stbrides.com).

96 St Helen's Bishopsgate

Christ's message in the financial district

Work in the banking business 'can represent a challenge for Christians who want to live for Jesus', says the website of the church without overstating the case. For Bible groups and midday talks, St Helen's Bishopsgate opens its doors to employees from the flashy high-rises of financial institutions that overshadow it. Externally, the church looks squat and modest, which makes the light-filled, spacious interior all the more surprising. St Helen's has two naves, as the church of a nunnery was added to the existing parish church in 1210. After the dissolution of the convent in 1538, the division between the two parts was removed to make a wide space whose brightness today is the result of IRA bombs that destroyed the dark Victorian stained glass in 1992 and 1993.

It is worth taking time to explore St Helen's, as it has been at the heart of a prosperous community for 800 years. In the Middle Ages, rich merchants, anxious to secure their salvation and the family reputation, embellished the church. A father of City finance lies in a sumptuous tomb in the north-east corner: Sir Thomas Gresham (1519–79), who founded the London Exchange. The Renaissance monument to Sir William Pickering, English ambassador to Spain († 1574), is even more imposing. Framed by iron railings and marble columns, he lies with hands folded in prayer, wearing armour on his chest, delicate wrist ruffs and a trunk hose that looks as if it had been pumped up.

As St Helen's is not only a piece of preserved heritage but a lively meeting place for Christians, workaday items stand among the ostentatious tombs in quirky contrast: plain plastic chairs, chequered tablecloths and coat stands on wheels. To prevent utilitarian fittings from spoiling the church more than necessary, the legally required notice 'Fire Exit' has been painted on the carved wooden doors in beautiful golden lettering.

Address Great St Helen's, EC3A 6AT | **Getting there** Tube to Liverpool Street (Central, Circle, Hammersmith & City, Metropolitan Line) | **Hours** See www.st-helens.org.uk | **Tip** Diners in the Duck and Waffle (110 Bishopsgate, daily 7.30am–12.30am, reservations at duckandwaffle.com) look down on churches and banks from the 40th floor of the 202-metre Heron Tower. Given this location, the prices of the food are acceptable.

97 St John's Lodge Garden

A sequestered spot in Regent's Park

At the heart of one of London's largest parks, an enchanted garden with a surprisingly intimate character is hidden away. It originally belonged to St John's Lodge, which was built in 1819 as one of 50 houses that were intended to make Regent's Park the finest residential area in London. This was part of an ambitious project planned by John Nash, who laid out Regent Street at the same time. Nash built the grand terraces that still stand all around the park, with their views of the lake, trees and lawns, but only two of the planned 50 detached residences were completed.

After several changes of owner (it is now in the possession of the ruling family of Kuwait), St John's Lodge was bought in 1888 by the Marquis of Bute, who desired a garden 'suitable for meditation'. The secluded garden created for him became part of the public park 40 years later. To find it, go to the north-eastern segment of the park's Inner Circle and look out for an inconspicuous gate, behind which a path leads to St John's Lodge Garden.

Accurately clipped hedges and densely growing shrubs divide the garden into a succession of separate spaces. In the summer months, the flower beds are full of luxuriant blooms in harmonious colour schemes – for the pink-to-purple spectrum, for example, roses are planted next to campanula, matching lupins and cranesbill. The geometric layout of the garden frames views of the Lodge. Bowers covered with climbing plants provide shade, elegant seats invite visitors to settle down for the afternoon with a good book and, just as the Marquis of Bute wished, works of art furnish food for contemplation. A sculpture on the round pond depicts the youth Hylas, whom water nymphs are pulling down into the depths. According to the Greek myth, Hylas never resurfaced – and this garden is a spot from which you will not want to re-emerge into the noise of London.

Address Inner Circle, Regent's Park, NW8 | **Getting there** Tube to Regent's Park (Bakerloo Line) | **Hours** Daily 7am until dusk | **Tip** The Regent's Bar & Kitchen within the Inner Circle adjoining the wonderful Queen Mary's Garden serves afternoon tea, snacks and main meals (Mon–Fri 9am–6pm, Sat & Sun 8am–7pm).

98 St Pancras Station

An engineering miracle based on beer

Passengers arriving at St Pancras International on the Eurostar trains from Paris are greeted by a masterpiece of Victorian architecture, an aesthetic and engineering marvel. The golden age of railway construction was coming to an end in Britain when St Pancras Station was opened in 1868. The engineer William Henry Barlow was therefore able to benefit from the experience of many predecessors. Whereas trains steaming into the neighbouring King's Cross Station entered two parallel sheds with a width of 32 metres each, Barlow designed a roof with a single span of 74.8 metres, a new record that was only exceeded 20 years later. Barlow's innovative construction of 25 pointed arches of iron, braced by lateral girders hidden beneath the tracks, enabled him to build a single span without an extensive web of trusses below the main arches, which would have detracted from the clean lines of the roof.

To the north of the station lies the Regent's Canal, which the railway had to cross in a tunnel or on a bridge. As the gradient that a tunnel would have required presented problems for locomotives of that era, Barlow opted for a bridge, with the consequence that the tracks reached the station above street level. The space beneath them was used by the Midland Railway to store up to 100,000 beer barrels, as part of the company's business was to supply beer from Burton-on-Trent for London's insatiable thirst. The distance between the 800 cast-iron columns that support the tracks was a multiple of the size of a 36-gallon barrel. The roof arches are twice as far apart as the columns. Thus the breathtaking architectural space of St Pancras is based on the Burton beer barrel.

The renovation and alteration of the station for its reopening in 2007 restored the architecture to its old glory and allowed light to flood through the roof again. The beer store is now the arrivals hall for the Eurostar service.

Address Euston Road, N1C 4QL | Getting there Tube to King's Cross-St Pancras (Circle, Hammersmith & City, Metropolitan, Northern, Victoria Line) | Tip The station hotel at St Pancras, designed by George Gilbert Scott, is one of the very finest examples of Victorian architecture. The restaurant in the old ticket office gives an impression of its superb interiors.

99 __ Three Mills Island

Grinding grain with tidal power

A large area in the Lea valley between the Thames and the Olympic site was an ugly wasteland left behind by the chemical industry until a few years ago. Thanks to the cleaning-up and greening of the waterways here, an older industrial location, which is anything but ugly, has more pleasant surroundings.

Mills on the site now called Three Mills Island were recorded in the Domesday Book in 1086. They probably used tide power even at this early date. Rising water flowed into a reservoir and was retained there by sluice gates. It then flowed back into the river during ebb tide, turning water wheels. As this technology was perfected over centuries, by 1938 the mill wheels could be operated for seven or eight hours during each tide. In the 16th century the components of gunpowder were being milled here, as well as flour. Huge demand for gin in the 18th century kept the wheels turning to grind the required grain. In 1776 the Huguenot Daniel Bisson rebuilt House Mill in its present form, and 40 years later Clock Mill was added. The latter still has its clock turret and distinctive roofs above the drying floors. The grain was used to distil alcohol on site. Clock Mill operated until 1952 and is now part of London's largest film and TV studios.

In House Mill, possibly the world's largest tidal mill, water wheels with a diameter of six metres drove 14 pairs of millstones in 1880. Production ceased in 1941, but the River Lea Tidal Mill Trust is restoring the remaining four wheels and machinery with the aim of generating electricity. Visitors can admire the wonderful brick architecture of the mill and adjacent miller's house, home to a café and education centre, and follow the processes from delivery of grain by boat to sacks of flour ready for collection. This is an industrial monument of the first rank, with a history reaching back more than 900 years.

Address Three Mills Island, E3 3DU | Getting there Tube to Bromley-by-Bow (District, Hammersmith & City Line) | Hours House Mill May–Oct Sun 11am–4pm | Tip Waterside paths lead north to the Olympic site and the park that is being created on the River Lea, or south to the Thames. For routes see www.visitleevalley.org.uk.

100   The Tibetan Peace Garden

A mandala at the cannon's mouth

What's the most suitable place for laying out a peace garden? London's answer to the question may come as a surprise: the Tibetan Peace Garden has found its home in the park in front of the Imperial War Museum, where a massive artillery piece greets visitors at the main entrance. On the green space in front of the museum, the Dalai Lama consecrated the garden that his Tibet Foundation presented to the British people in 1999.

The first thing that comes into view when approaching the garden is the stone 'Language Pillar'. This is modelled on the Sho Pillar of the Potala Palace in Lhasa. On its four sides a message from the Dalai Lama has been inscribed in Tibetan, English, Chinese and Hindi. The text refers to 'the immeasurable human suffering and environmental destruction' of the 20th century, warns that the survival of humankind depends on harmonious coexistence, and describes the garden as a monument to the courage and commitment to peace of the people of Tibet.

A path leads from this pillar to the inner circle of the garden, representing the Wheel of Dharma. At the centre, cast in bronze, is the Kalachakra Mandala, which is said to confer blessings on all who see it. Around the mandala are eight meditation seats for the Noble Eightfold Path of Buddhism: the right view, thought, speech, action, livelihood, effort, mindfulness and concentration. Plants from Tibet and its region are cultivated in the flower beds round about. Four Western-style sculptures at the edge of the circle symbolise the elements of air, fire, earth and water. The fifth element in Buddhism, space, is the open area of the circle. These works of art are linked by a pergola on which climbing plants grow – some from the Himalayas, others, such as honeysuckle native to Britain. In this way, the garden embodies the idea of reconciliation between East and West.

Address St George's Road, SE1 6ER | **Getting there** Tube to Elephant & Castle (Northern, Bakerloo Line), then a short walk north-west along St George's Road; from Waterloo Station it's a 10-minute walk south along Waterloo Road | **Tip** The Imperial War Museum, equally recommended for pacifists and fans of military hardware, belies its name through a sensitive approach to the topic of humanity and war (daily 10am–6pm, admission free).

101 Tower Bridge Wharf

A clear view of the river

Walking east along St Katharine's Way, you see a round building on the right-hand side shortly before reaching Wapping High Street. Pass through the gate to see an open paved area with seats on the banks of the river. Here you can gain a different impression of the Thames than in Westminster, as it changes from an embanked and bridged city river hemmed in by large buildings to a major commercial waterway on course for the sea. The Thames gradually becomes wider, and the rise and fall of tides is more noticeable. Passenger boats passing at speed and the currents of tide and river send waves slapping against the quay. Wind ruffles the choppy water and makes it sparkle in the sunshine. This spot, Tower Bridge Wharf, is a fine place to linger, whether the sky reflected in the Thames is blue or grey, thanks to a wonderful view along the water and across to the south bank.

Directly opposite lies Butler's Wharf, where the largest tea warehouse in the world has been converted to luxury flats. Further to the right, the architectural jumble of new and old is almost startling: the brutal 1970s' concrete tower of Guy's Hospital, the tilted egg-shape of City Hall and the piercingly self-promotional Shard line up one behind the other next to the Gothic silhouette of Tower Bridge. Turning to look along the north bank, you can see The Monument and St Paul's Cathedral with the British Telecom tower in the background.

After a rest at Tower Bridge Wharf, follow the Thames Path east through the redeveloped Docklands. A short way downstream, brightly coloured pennants flutter on traditional river barges. They are moored in front of new waterfront housing, past which the path leads to the Hermitage Riverside Memorial Garden. Here, in an area that suffered heavy bombing, flower beds and sculptures commemorate the civilians who died in the Second World War.

Address St Katherine's Way, E1W 1UR | Getting there Tube to Tower Hill (Circle, District Line) | Hours Daily 8am–11pm | Tip The Dickens Inn at St Katharine Docks is a tourist magnet, but good beer in a historic timber building makes it worth stopping there (Mon–Sat 11am–11pm, Sun noon–10.30pm).

102 The Trafalgar Tavern

Maritime tradition on the Greenwich Meridian

Naval themes take pride of place in Greenwich, where the National Maritime Museum and the Royal Observatory stand on the line of zero longitude. A handsome Thames-side pub matches this tradition perfectly. The Trafalgar Tavern was built in 1837. It's not only the name that honours Lord Nelson's great victory – the admiral himself stands outside in a jaunty pose, cast in bronze, his empty right sleeve tucked into his coat. Wearing a bicorn hat and medals on his chest, he turns his back on drinkers in the beer garden, directing a resolute gaze towards the north, as if planning to demolish the high-rise buildings across the river with a full broadside.

The Trafalgar Tavern has an imposing riverside façade, with rounded bay windows, Ionic columns and a flagpole. The historic sash windows and balconies are fronted by cast-iron balustrades. At low tide a small shingle beach is revealed in front of the tavern, but waves slap against the outer wall at high water. A patriotic pub sign displays the Union Jack, the royal arms and the navy's Blue Ensign.

The stylish interior more than lives up to the external impression of quality. There are fine mirrors and maritime pictures on the walls, plaster decoration on the ceiling, and crystal chandeliers in the restaurant. Drinkers in the bar area sink into comfortable armchairs, and can warm themselves by the open fire in winter. In the 19th century, the prime minister and cabinet members came here for an annual whitebait dinner when Parliament rose for the summer recess. Whitebait – various kinds of young fish, mainly herring – remains on the menu, alongside hearty pub dishes such as fish and chips or leg of lamb. A huge selection of different kinds of rum upholds the traditions of the Royal Navy. Guests who arrive early enough to get a window seat can watch traffic passing on the river and the light dancing on the surface of the water as they enjoy their beer, coffee or rum.

Address Park Row, Greenwich, SE10 9NW, +44 (0)20 3887 9886,
www.trafalgartavern.co.uk | Getting there DLR to Cutty Sark or a boat to Greenwich, then
a five-minute walk east on the river bank | Hours Mon–Thu noon–11pm, Fri noon–1am,
Sat 9–1am, Sun 9am–11pm; food served daily until 9pm | Tip The Fan Museum provides
charming insights into ladies' fashion in bygone days (12 Crooms Hill, Greenwich,
www.thefanmuseum.org.uk; Tue–Sat 11am–5pm, Sun noon–5pm).

103 Trellick Tower

The rehabilitation of an architectural villain

Let's start with some straightforward facts. The Royal Borough of Kensington and Chelsea commissioned the Hungarian-born Ernö Goldfinger (1902–1987) to design Trellick Tower. A separate tower for lifts and utilities is joined to the lobbies of the 98-metre-high main tower in the Brutalist style on every third storey. After completion in 1972, 217 flats on 31 floors were rented to council tenants.

Goldfinger's character and work have not always been seen in sober, factual terms. As a student in Paris, he admired the Modernist architecture of Mies van der Rohe and Le Corbusier. In the 1930s he married an English heiress, moved to London, and built himself a home in Willow Road in Hampstead that is now regarded as an icon of early Modernism in England and belongs to the National Trust. Its construction required the demolition of older houses. The author Ian Fleming, a neighbour, was incensed at this, and his dislike of the architect increased when a golf partner described Goldfinger as choleric and humourless. Thus Fleming found a title for the eighth James Bond novel and the name of his most infamous villain.

Trellick Tower was long regarded as a monstrosity, an example of disastrous housing causing social evils. In its first years, the building was notorious for drug dealing and violent crime. Changes for the better began in the 1980s through security measures and tenants' right to buy their council flats. Some privatised units in the block now change hands at prices of up to 800,000 pounds. Today, glossing over problems such as the heat-leaking façade, estate agents praise 'fashionable accommodation with an unimpeded view of London from the 30th floor (with lift and concierge)'. In the 1990s, the conservation authorities discovered the aesthetic merits of Brutalism, and sealed Goldfinger's rehabilitation by giving Trellick Tower a grade-two listing.

Address Golborne Road, W10 5NY | Getting there Tube to Westbourne Park (Hammersmith & City Line) | Hours By appointment. Search the internet for estate agents who have a flat in Trellick Tower on their books, and pretend to be a potential purchaser. | Tip Portobello Road, dreadfully overcrowded for the Saturday market, is a pleasant place to shop on weekdays. Golborne Road and the northern part of Ladbroke Grove with their antique and design shops are a mix of chic and shabby.

104_ Tyburn Convent
A shrine to Roman Catholic martyrs

Near the roaring junction of Edgware Road and Bayswater Road is a place of tranquillity and meditation. It is no coincidence that the convent is here: the village of Tyburn, where Marble Arch now stands, was a site for executions from the Middle Ages until 1783. From 1571 the hangings took place on 'Tyburn Tree', a gallows in the form of a horizontal triangle with three supports, large enough for the execution of more than 20 people at the same time. An estimated 50,000 died here, surrounded by jeering crowds who expected them to be defiant and spirited in the face of death.

Not only criminals were hanged. Tyburn Convent commemorates 350 Roman Catholic martyrs. The first of them were sent to Tyburn for refusing to recognise Henry VIII as head of the Anglican church. After a brief pause under Henry's Catholic daughter Mary I (reigned 1553–1558), persecution continued under Elizabeth I. Loyalty to Rome was seen as disobedience to the monarch and thus as treachery. The Catholics who died at Tyburn in the reigns of Elizabeth and her successors include two who were canonised: the Jesuit priest St Edmund Campion († 1581) and St Oliver Plunkett, Archbishop of Armagh († 1681, the last person who was condemned to die as a martyr on Tyburn Tree).

Martyrs' coats of arms line the walls of the plain chapel of Tyburn Convent, where nuns have lived according to the rule of St Benedict since 1901. They sing Mass seven times daily and keep silent vigil round the clock in adoration of the Blessed Sacrament, separated by a metal grille from the faithful who come in from the street to pray. Three times each day the nuns take visitors to the crypt, where relics such as bones, a fingernail and hair of the martyrs are kept. Outside the convent, traffic thunders along, the super-rich live in their mansions with a view of Hyde Park, and shoppers seek their consumer heaven on Oxford Street.

Address 8–12 Hyde Park Place, W2 2LJ | Getting there Tube to Marble Arch (Central Line) | Hours Daily 6.30am–8.30pm, tours of the shrine daily 3.30pm | Tip It is worth taking a closer look at Marble Arch, even though many of the planned sculptures were left off to save costs. Originally the ceremonial entrance to Buckingham Palace, it was moved to its present site in 1851.

105__Waterloo Bridge

One of the best views along the Thames

A charming pop song of the 1960s, 'Waterloo Sunset' by The Kinks, celebrates the beauty of the Thames. Two lovers meet at Waterloo Station and cross the bridge: 'As long as I gaze on Waterloo sunset, I am in paradise'. In 1802, not far away on Westminster Bridge, William Wordsworth wrote that 'Earth has not anything to show more fair'. The poet did not know that Waterloo Bridge would soon be built on an even more advantageous site, the mid-point of a bend in the river, which means that it gives passers-by a view of both Westminster to the south-west and the City of London to the east.

This first Waterloo Bridge, whose nine arches spanned the Thames from 1817, inspired painters and writers. It was a motif for John Constable and Claude Monet. A stage play named Waterloo Bridge, first performed in 1930 and filmed no less than three times, told the story of a soldier and a dancer who met on the bridge during a bombing raid in the First World War.

The second bridge, which still stands, was designed by Sir Giles Gilbert Scott and completed in 1942. The architect of the famous telephone box and two striking buildings on the banks of the Thames, the power stations in Bankside (now the Tate Modern) and Battersea, failed to create a beautiful bridge, but the panorama on both sides makes up for this. Close by are Somerset House (to the left on the north bank, when looking towards the City) and the National Theatre (on the south bank opposite). Further east St Paul's Cathedral, The Monument and St Bride's Church rise with the bank towers of the financial district beyond them and to the right. From the other side of the bridge, facing Westminster, the eyes rove past the cultural institutions of the Southbank Centre towards the London Eye and right to the unmistakable silhouette of Parliament. To stand on this bridge, beneath a wide sky and above a broad river, is to feel that London is truly a great city.

Address Waterloo Bridge | **Getting there** Tube to Temple (Circle, District Line) | **Tip**
You also get a wonderful view from the two pedestrian river crossings on either side of the
Hungerford Railway Bridge, to the south of Waterloo Bridge.

106___ The Westbourne

The stream that flows through a Tube station

Subterranean rivers are, needless to say, invisible. There is an exception to this in the Tube station at Sloane Square, where the Westbourne crosses the tracks above the heads of passengers waiting on the platforms. They hear no splashes and see no water, as the stream flows through a closed iron trough. Nevertheless, to look up at the black-painted underside of the aqueduct is a rare opportunity to glimpse one of the many watercourses that otherwise lie unseen beneath the city streets.

Some 21 small rivers and streams flow into the Thames within the boundaries of Greater London. Some of them run through the suburbs above ground, but in the city centre they all disappeared from view long ago. The Walbrook, for example, on whose banks the history of London began 2,000 years ago, was covered up in the 1440s. The Tyburn passes beneath Buckingham Palace. The Fleet River, which rises on Hampstead Heath and enters the Thames near Black friars Bridge, was hidden underground in the 18th century, although the quays on its banks were commercially useful, because it gave off an intolerable stench.

The source of the Westbourne is on the west side of Hampstead Heath. It flows, already below the earth, through Kilburn and Maida Vale towards Paddington Station, where its course is parallel to Westbourne Terrace. From 1731 its waters fed a new lake in Hyde Park, The Serpentine, but became so polluted that in the 19th century they had to be diverted through a channel around the north side of the lake. After flowing beneath Belgravia, the Westbourne makes its brief appearance at Sloane Square Station, then continues below Holbein Place and the gardens of the Royal Hospital to its outlet near Chelsea Bridge. By looking from the bridge at low tide, it is possible to see the main outfall a short distance upstream, and two smaller ones on the downstream side.

Address Sloane Square | Getting there Tube to Sloane Square (Circle, District Line) |
Tip The Tyburn Angling Society (www.ediblegeography.com/the-tyburn-angling-society)
proposes, not seriously, restoring another lost river to its natural state. This would involve
demolishing Buckingham Palace.

107 __ The White Building
Art and pizza by the canal

On the east bank of the canal, in Queen Elizabeth Park, site of the 2012 Olympic Games, everything has been carefully planned: paths, playgrounds, works of art, lawns and flower beds, sports facilities. Although this has been well done, it is a liberating feeling to cross the old bridge to the less orderly, more creative district of Hackney Wick, where the grass grows as it pleases from cracks in the paving and art is not necessarily the result of a public commission, but appears overnight on the walls.

Where White Post Lane crosses the canal, Clarnico, a maker of mint creams and chocolate, built a roasting plant for cocoa beans in 1897. Later a printworks moved in. In the new millennium it became The White Building, a 'creative lab' with event spaces, studios and residencies for artists who explored the themes of technology and sustainability. While major construction companies worked on the Olympic stadium across the canal, here the architects engaged local builders for the conversion. They hung red nets filled with sheep's wool from the ceilings for insulation and acoustic softening, and created access to a sheltered area on the canal bank that is now occupied by outdoor seating for the Crate Brewery, which runs a pub and pizzeria on the site.

The brewery furnished the ground floor with recycled materials. The bar is made from railway sleepers, the benches from pallets. Scaffolding planks were used to make tables bed springs for the lamp fittings. Here in hipster Hackney the brewery produces, needless to say, a range of craft beers, from IPA to stout. They are just right for washing down pizza in trendy flavours such as sage and truffle, or Kashmiri with Indian spices. Diners on the terrace can watch passing narrowboats, rowers and paddleboarders, and look across the water to sprayed art on the wall of another surviving part of the Clarnico factory.

Address Unit 7, Queens Yard, Hackney Wick, E9 5EN, www.spacestudios.org.uk; Crate Brewery +44 (0)754 769 5841, www.cratebrewery.com | Getting there Overground to Hackney Wick, then five minutes' walk via White Post Lane | Hours Crate Brewery Sun–Thu noon–11pm, Fri–Sat until midnight | Tip A short walk north on the canal are more places to eat and drink, e.g. Grow, a restaurant and bar with a space for music and art events (www.growhackney.co.uk).

108__ Whitechapel Gallery
Art for all and a golden tree

When the Whitechapel Gallery opened in 1901, its founders' aim was to make culture, especially contemporary art, accessible to the poor of the East End. The façade of the gallery expressed this spirit of innovation and idealism thanks to its unusual asymmetrical design with Art Nouveau influence by Charles Harrison Townsend. The mosaic frieze that was planned for the recess between the two towers was never carried out, but the motif of the Tree of Life on terracotta panels on the lower parts of the towers symbolised growth, learning and renewal.

Since its early days, the gallery has taken a pioneering role. In 1938 it exhibited Picasso's Guernica in response to a nascent fascist movement that deliberately provoked the many Jewish and left-wing inhabitants of Whitechapel. In 1956 the exhibition 'This Is Tomorrow' was the first in England to show Pop Art. Jackson Pollock, Mark Rothko and Frida Kahlo were first presented to the London art scene in this gallery, which also promoted British artists such as Gilbert & George. A well-known contemporary artist who has lived near Whitechapel Gallery for 25 years, Rachel Whiteread, has now remodelled its façade.

Much of Whiteread's work involves making casts of large and small objects, thus creating modern sculptures with historical references. She first came to prominence in 1993 with a full-sized cast of the interior of a complete house in the East End. For the Whitechapel Gallery, she placed four casts of the existing windows between the towers, and added golden decoration derived from the terracotta Trees of Life: bronze replicas of their branches and leaves scattered across the recess and the towers. Whiteread thus refers to the history of the gallery, which continues to fulfil its original purpose of bringing art to east London, and is also worth visiting for its café and bookshop.

Address 77–82 Whitechapel High Street, E1 7QX | Getting there Tube to Aldgate
East (District, Hammersmith & City Line) | Hours Tue–Sun 11am–6pm | Tip Over
150 galleries and museums in East London, including the Whitechapel Gallery, open
until 9pm on the first Thursday of the month. Most of the exhibitions, performances,
concerts and guided tours are free (www.firstthursdays.co.uk).

109 Wilton's Music Hall

Bare boards, crumbling plaster

This small theatre has survived everything that fate could throw at it: a fire in 1877, the Blitz of 1940–1941, slum clearances in the 1960s and decades of neglect. From the street, there is no sign of a theatre – only a row of terraced houses with traces of red paint on a shabby façade. The decay becomes clearer when you enter the hallway, where the floorboards are bare and the brick walls have lost their plaster. In the auditorium beyond, delicate spiral columns support the galleries. After a short time, as your eyes get used to the darkness, the remains of stucco decoration and gilding become visible. Welcome to Wilton's Music Hall, the last of its kind!

Nineteenth-century music-hall shows comprehended everything that could make the public laugh, cry or cheer: from singers and comedians to acrobats, ventriloquists, dancers and sword-swallowers. At Wilton's this entertainment developed from sing-songs in a seamen's tavern in the 1740s. A concert hall built behind the pub in 1839 was enlarged 20 years later by John Wilton. He constructed a high stage to give the audience a clear view, even over the top hats of gentlemen who came from the West End to indulge in some low life, and adorned the room with mirrors, crystal chandeliers and a 'sunlight' with 100 gas jets to make everything sparkle. Oscar Wilde's Picture of Dorian Gray describes how such a light 'flamed like a monstrous dahlia with petals of yellow fire'.

The days of glory were soon over. Splendid new theatres supplanted simple halls like Wilton's, which became a Methodist mission and finally a storehouse. In 1971 it was listed as the only surviving first-generation music hall. Following years of fundraising and publicity work, restoration and careful modernisation were completed in 2015, making Wilton's fit for operation as a theatre without spoiling its morbid charm. Go there after dark and listen: does the laughter of past times still echo?

Address 1 Grace's Alley, Ensign Street, E1 8JB, www.wiltons.org.uk | Getting there Tube to Tower Hill (Circle, District Line), or DLR to Tower Gateway | Hours For musical and dramatic performances, food and drink in the Mahogany Bar see website | Tip Five minutes along Cable Street is the Cable Street Mural (1983), commemorating a battle in 1936, when locals stopped a march by the British Union of Fascists.

110 The Wimbledon Windmill

A survival from rustic village days

Greater London covers more than 600 square miles. An insatiable giant, it has swallowed up many villages and countless acres of farm-land. Here and there, traces of the past agricultural use of the terrain survive, including no fewer than nine windmills. One of them occupies a windy height on Wimbledon Common.

The mill was constructed in 1817 to supply the surrounding communities. It was the work of a carpenter, which is why originally only the octagonal base was brick-built: he used wood for the upper parts. The mill ground grain into flour until 1864, when the owner of the land, the fifth Earl Spencer (his great-great-grandson, the ninth earl, is brother to the late Princess Diana), applied to convert the common into a private park and place a new country house on the site of the mill. Following an inquiry, permission was refused – a decision that set an important precedent for the preservation of common land. A board of conservators was created to protect Wimbledon Common, and Earl Spencer received an annual rent in compensation. The windmill became a home for six families with the addition of a new brick upper floor and chimneys. Further rebuilding work took place in 1893, and the mill was inhabited until 1975.

Today, it houses a museum. Moving models explain the construction and technology of windmills from early times through to modern wind turbines. The Wimbledon mill is an example of hollow-post construction: an iron shaft within the central post transmitted the power downwards from the sails to the grinding machinery on the first floor. The sails have been restored, but no grain is ground today, except by hand for demonstration purposes, as the miller removed the wheels and shafts in 1864. One room has been furnished to illustrate the private accommodation in the period around 1870.

Address Windmill Road, SW19 5NR, www.wimbledonwindmill.org.uk | **Getting there** Bus 93 between Wimbledon and Putney stations, both reached by train from Waterloo, stops at Windmill Road | **Hours** End-Mar–Oct Sat 2–5pm, Sun 11–5pm | **Tip** The Windmill Tearooms serves hot meals until 3.30pm (Mon–Fri 9am–5.15pm, Sat 9am–5.45pm, Sun 9am–6.15pm).

112 — Ye Olde Mitre
A well-hidden pub

A pub that is so difficult to find, is closed at weekends, and yet has stayed in business for centuries must have something special. To discover its secret, turn left from Holborn Circus into Hatton Garden and look out for a narrow passage by the fifth building on the right. Or pass through the gates at the end of Ely Place and turn left into the passage. In front of a façade of wood and bull's-eye window panes, the sign Ye Olde Mitre depicts a bishop's hat and names the year 1546, when a tavern first started to serve beer on the grounds of a bishop's palace.

The present building dates from 1773. Its furnishings of wooden panelling, bench seats around the walls and spacious armchairs are a mere 80 years old, but convincingly create the atmosphere of an ancient tavern, especially after a pint or two: the Mitre is known for the good quality of its ales, which are drawn from hand pumps at the bar between two of the lounges. In the back room, water jugs hang from the ceiling and wall lights provide subdued illumination. The front room has a fireplace and a real historical curiosity: the trunk of a cherry tree that once marked the property boundary. According to tradition, Queen Elizabeth I danced around this tree with her court favourite, Sir Christopher Hatton. Whether this really happened or not, it is known that Elizabeth put pressure on the Bishop of Ely to sell part of the palace to Hatton, and liked to visit her courtier there.

The only remaining part of the palace is its chapel, St Etheldreda on Ely Place. The gates and guardhouse at the end of this private road are a reminder that it belonged to a closed precinct under the bishops' jurisdiction. The entrance to Ye Olde Mitre harks back to London's past, when the city was a warren of dark alleys and hidden courtyards. Good beer, filling pies and loyal customers ensure that it will also be part of London's future.

Address 1 Ely Court, Ely Place, EC1N 6SJ | Getting there Tube to Chancery Lane (Central Line) | Hours Mon–Fri noon–11pm | Tip St Etheldreda's (open for prayer and Mass, see www.stetheldreda.com) on Ely Place was built around 1290. It has been a Roman Catholic church since restoration in 1873, and gained new stained-glass windows in the 1950s following war damage.

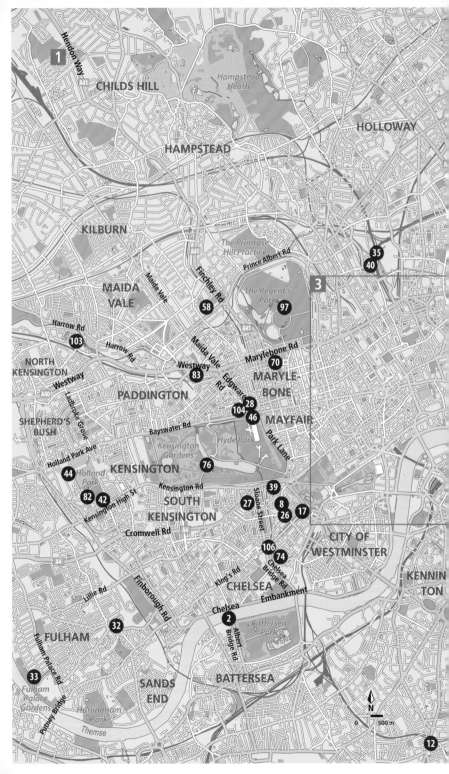

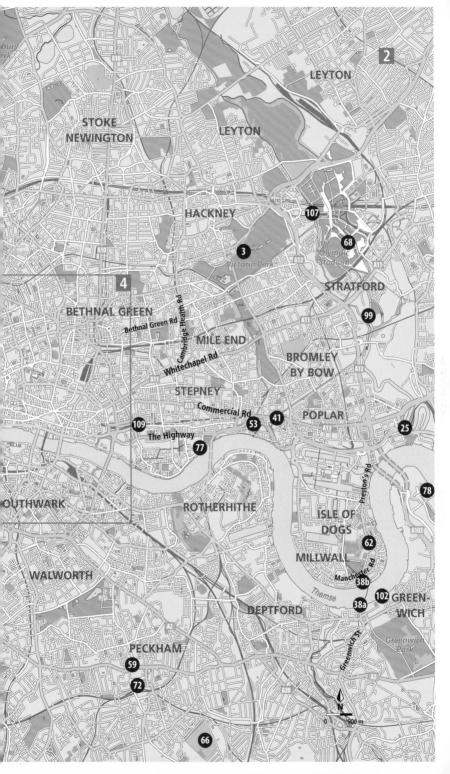

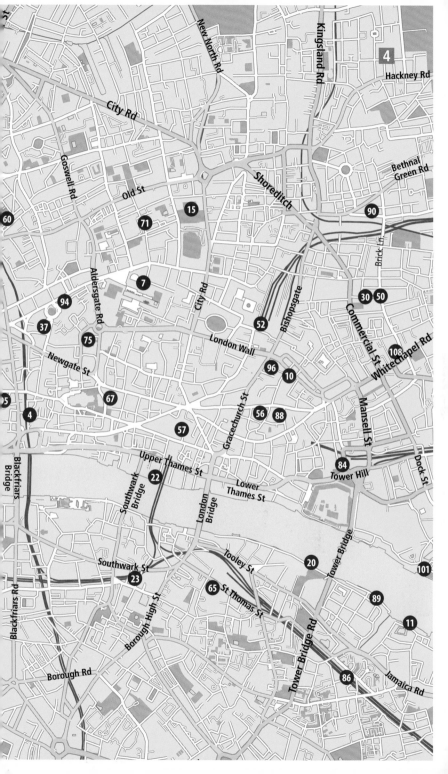

Nicola Perry, Daniel Reiter
33 Walks in London
That You Shouldn't Miss
ISBN 978-3-95451-886-9

Kirstin von Glasow
111 Gardens in London
That You Shouldn't Miss
ISBN 978-3-7408-0143-4

Laura Richards, Jamie Newson
111 London Pubs and Bars
That You Shouldn't Miss
ISBN 978-3-7408-0893-8

Emma Rose Barber,
Benedict Flett
111 Churches in London
That You Shouldn't Miss
ISBN 978-3-7408-0901-0

Ed Glinert, Marc Zakian
111 Places in London's East
End That You Shouldn't Miss
ISBN 978-3-7408-0752-8

Solange Berchemin,
Martin Dunford, Karin Tearle
111 Places in Greenwich
That You Shouldn't Miss
ISBN 978-3-7408-1107-5

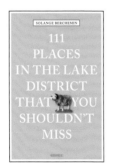

Solange Berchemin
111 Places in the Lake District
That You Shouldn't Miss
ISBN 978-3-7408-0378-0

Rob Ganley, Ian Williams
111 Places in Coventry
That You Shouldn't Miss
ISBN 978-3-7408-1044-3

Martin Booth, Barbara Evripidou
111 Places in Bristol
That You Shouldn't Miss
ISBN 978-3-7408-0898-3

Kim Revill, Alesh Compton
111 Places in Leeds
That You Shouldn't Miss
ISBN 978-3-7408-0754-2

Julian Treuherz,
Peter de Figueiredo
111 Places in Manchester
That You Shouldn't Miss
ISBN 978-3-7408-0753-5

Julian Treuherz,
Peter de Figueiredo
111 Places in Liverpool
That You Shouldn't Miss
ISBN 978-3-95451-769-5

Michael Glover,
Richard Anderson
111 Places in Sheffield
That You Shouldn't Miss
ISBN 978-3-7408-0022-2

Katherine Bebo, Oliver Smith
111 Places in Poole
That You Shouldn't Miss
ISBN 978-3-7408-0598-2

Alexandra Loske
111 Places in Brighton and
Lewes That You Shouldn't Miss
ISBN 978-3-7408-0255-4

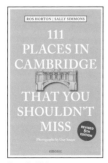

Rosalind Horton,
Sally Simmons, Guy Snape
111 Places in Cambridge
That You Shouldn't Miss
ISBN 978-3-7408-0147-2

Justin Postlethwaite
111 Places in Bath
That You Shouldn't Miss
ISBN 978-3-7408-0146-5

Gillian Tait
111 Places in Edinburgh
That You Shouldn't Miss
ISBN 978-3-95451-883-8

We are grateful to the following friends who gave us invaluable support during the work on this book: David Brock, Oliver Bryce, Patricia Carroll, Stuart Condie, Maria Ejsmont-Rybicka, André Gren, Jamilla Lord, Simon Lord, Tina Papenfuss, Simon Prior, Ryszard Rybicki, Tony Sharp, Caryl Varty, Larissa Weeke.

John Sykes, was born in Southport, Lancashire, studied in Oxford and Manchester and lived in London before moving to Germany and making his home in Cologne. He has written and translated books about London, including a Sherlock Holmes mystery, and is the author of several travel guides about the British Isles.

Birgit Weber studied in Aachen and lives in Cologne. She has worked on many book projects, including several about London. For more than 30 years she has been travelling to Britain and is regularly in London. The city fascinates her every time, because there is always something new to discover.